The Mathematical Toolbox

Rosamond Welchman-Tischler

Cuisenaire Company of America, Inc.
P.O. Box 5026
White Plains, NY 10602-5026

Acknowledgement

Work for this book was partially supported by the Brooklyn College Mathematics Teacher Enhancement Program, funded by the National Science Foundation (Teacher Enhancement Program). Many teachers with whom I have worked both in this program and in other contexts have contributed to the book by working through the problems themselves and with their classes. I would especially like to thank Dorothy Geddes for her support and careful reading of the entire manuscript. Michael Epstein and Irene Fortunato were also very helpful in providing constructive comments. Finally, I cannot imagine a more energetic, helpful and thoughtful editor than Doris Hirschhorn.

Design/computer illustration: Nancy R. Naft
Hand-drawn illustrations: Sam Tomasello

Table of Contents

INTRODUCTION

Rationale

Picture a child absorbed in a mathematical challenge, excitedly explaining a new approach or result to a friend, and exclaiming joyously when a solution is reached. All children deserve such experiences – the challenge and enjoyment of tackling new and interesting mathematics problems, working hard on them, and finding and sharing solutions. These experiences can be the motivation for and heart of learning the mathematical tools which constitute much of the traditional mathematics curriculum. In real life, few problems can be understood and solved neatly and quickly. To be prepared for their futures, children should have experiences of sustained investigations, where they can share ideas with others and learn to appreciate that there are often varied routes to success, sometimes more than one "correct" solution, and sometimes no solution.

Mathematical learning has many aspects. In the past, children's school mathematics experience was often dictated by the content of standardized tests, and was largely based on memory of computational skills, vocabulary, formulas, etc. However our modern world presents new challenges – complex problems requiring new and creative solutions – which have given rise to calls for a broader view of the mathematics curriculum. Lower level thinking skills are now perceived as the tools, the building blocks, out of which a much richer mathematical experience should be built, using higher order thinking skills such as reasoning, analysis, synthesis and evaluation. The National Council of Teachers of Mathematics has published two documents, *Curriculum and Evaluation Standards for School Mathematics*, and *Professional Standards for Teaching Mathematics*, which summarize and exemplify these trends.

Children's mathematical learning is not tightly sequenced. Teachers usually find in their classrooms children with many different levels of mathematical skill, types of thinking, self-confidence, and ability to sustain work on a problem. Some children with excellent memories excel on certain tasks, such as computation, yet are thrown by a non-routine problem. Such children, who may do well on multiple choice memory-dominated tests, sorely need more exposure to problems requiring higher order thinking skills. On the other hand, some children who are creative mathematical thinkers may be hampered by their lack of computational skills, which sometimes dooms them to a remedial curriculum based on low-level thinking skills. Such children may be sparked by a tough challenge that motivates them to learn the skills they lack.

This book provides a collection of mathematical challenges, arranged thematically and sequentially. Teachers can use this collection as a toolbox, helping them to match non-routine problems to their students' diverse abilities. A given type of challenge is interpreted at many different skill levels, and at least one in each set should be accessible to any child in elementary or junior high school. This sequential presentation of problems illustrates the continuity of mathematics – how the curriculum at one grade level relates to what comes before and after. The discussion of the challenges indicates that a given context or material can be approached on many different levels, both of skills and of "levels of thinking." The emphasis in classroom discussion of mathematics should be on this diversity of strategies that children bring to a problem, and not solely on the "answer."

The Role of Manipulative Materials

One tool for exploring problems is manipulation of materials representing mathematical ideas. When problems are phrased in terms of a manipulative material, as are most of the challenges in this book, several things happen. First, children are naturally motivated, especially if the materials are visually attractive and pleasant to handle. Second, manipulatives can become a thinking tool, an embodiment of a child's reasoning. In fact, research of Jean Piaget indicates that the reasoning of many elementary school children, unlike that of adults, is tied to such physical embodiments. (However even adults may sometimes rely on manipulatives to express their thinking.) Third, moving materials around leaves no trace, as does a pencil, and thus is risk-free, allowing children to develop confidence in experimentation. Finally, certain manipulatives have an inherent mathematical structure, and so provide a good context for posing challenges requiring the student to identify the mathematical characteristics of the material. As children grow older and more capable of abstract thought, their use of manipulatives should be accompanied by appropriately more abstract verbal or symbolic language. Thus, manipulatives have a role in problem exploration at all levels of elementary and junior high school.

Format of Pages

This book contains thirty-five sets of challenges. Each set is presented on one page, with eight problems labeled A through H. The eight challenges are related in some way, for example:

- they may all relate to the same manipulative material (Cuisenaire rods, geoboards, ...);
- they may all possess the same format, or call on the same mathematical process (finding what comes next in a pattern, ...);
- they may all relate to the same mathematics topic (graphing, fractions, ...);
- they may all be phrased in terms of a common theme (patchwork quilts, children's literature, ...).

The challenge sets are organized by these types of unifying characteristics. A brief summary of directions applying to all challenges on the page appears in the upper left corner. Each challenge is printed in a rectangle that can be enlarged on a copier to fill a standard sheet of paper and make a "mini-poster." The pages can also be duplicated directly for students.

The challenges are sequenced by level of difficulty, or by the grade placement of prerequisite mathematics topics in the curriculum. Roughly speaking, only skills usually developed in first grade are required for challenge A, second grade skills for challenge B, etc., up to eighth grade skills for challenge H. However, grade level suggestions should not be taken rigidly, because many challenges can be approached on different levels. Similar challenges might appear on different pages at different suggested levels. A question that may be quite routine for a student at one level might be non-routine for one who has had less experience with the topic. Some challenges may involve topics which are not normally required at the suggested grade level – this is intentional, giving students an opportunity to construct their own knowledge informally before the topic is formally presented to them.

On the back of each page is a commentary for teachers about the challenge set. This includes suggestions for teaching strategies, hints to get students moving on the challenges, ways to adapt the challenges and design new ones, "answers" where appropriate, and suggestions for further resources.

This collection is by no means exhaustive, and should be seen as a springboard to thinking about other manipulatives, processes, topics or themes in similar ways. The sets on manipulatives relate to some of the more commonly available commercial materials (Cuisenaire rods, pattern blocks, geoboards, tangrams, two-color counters, cubes, attribute sets, ...) as well as to a few materials which are readily available in "everyday life" (toothpicks, coins, playing cards, nuts, ...). The sets on processes or formats isolate techniques which are in fact also used in other challenge sets. These are adaptable to a wide range of topics in mathematics and in other curriculum areas. The mathematics topics selected for challenge sets lend themselves to interpretation at all levels of elementary and junior high school (estimation, counting, graphing, ...). Some topics which are not the focus of an entire challenge set nevertheless occur in many other sets related to material, process or theme (computation, two-dimensional geometry, ...). The themes chosen for challenge sets are merely representative, and will perhaps suggest ways that mathematics could be related to many other themes.

Ways to Use the Challenge Sets

The challenge sets can be used to enrich mathematics experiences in several ways. One challenge can be presented each week, possibly on Monday morning. It might be written on a corner of the chalkboard, or if it is more convenient, enlarged and displayed as a "mini-poster." Some teachers place an "answer box" below the challenge and encourage students to work on the challenge problem throughout the week, writing and putting their solutions in the box whenever they feel ready. Solutions are then read aloud and discussed at the end of the week. If a problem is particularly interesting to students, it can be adapted and/or repeated in a different guise in a later week. Some students may solve the challenge early in the week and want further challenges before the next Monday. You might mount some related problem or the next one or two in the sequence on file cards for such students.

For upper-grade students, who should be able to approach many of the challenges in a set, the entire page can be duplicated and given to them with the challenge to do what they can. Again, if this sheet is given out on a Monday, it might be discussed on a Friday. Students might also be asked to design another challenge to fit the set. In fact, challenge H might be replaced with a blank space, entitled "Your Own Challenge." If eight problems seem too many, consider duplicating an enlargement of one of the four corners of the page, giving just three or four problems instead.

The type of challenge represented in this collection should not be isolated from the rest of mathematics instruction. Challenges can motivate new topics, be used to develop and extend understanding, or review a topic previously covered. The commentary on the back of each set suggests many ways in which individual challenges can be modified, and it is hoped that this collection will be used as a "toolbox" for teachers who wish to incorporate higher level thinking skills throughout their teaching of mathematics.

General Teaching Strategies

The suggestions below apply to all of the challenges in this book, or in fact to any mathematical experiences designed to increase students' abilities and interest in exploring non-routine problems.

1. Allow time. Students think at different speeds. Insight into a problem may come suddenly and unpredictably. It is very discouraging for a student who is working on a problem to hear a solution suddenly and too soon. For most students, this robs them of the pleasure of finding their own solution, and also teaches them that it may be easier to wait until someone else gets the answer than to struggle for it themselves. Encourage students to write about their solutions, or to talk with the teacher about their strategies, rather than to talk with other students who are still working on the challenge.

2. Find a level of challenge where success is possible and difficulty is appropriate. Students need a certain amount of confidence to engage in mathematical investigations where the solution takes time. As children go through school, they sometimes lose faith in their ability to think about mathematical problems where they don't immediately know what to do. Older students may need some confidence-building challenges. If students are having a hard time getting started on a challenge, don't hesitate to offer an easier one. You can also provide hints, as suggested in the commentary on specific challenges in this book.

3. Promote communication. Children learn new strategies through seeing them modeled. Emphasize your interest in how children arrived at their solution, by having children express their thinking, either verbally to their classmates, or in writing. Investigating challenges need not be an individual experience. Children can be encouraged to think about the challenges as a group, and they may learn the value of working cooperatively – that different people can each contribute something to the group's understanding, and that a group may function better than any individual in it.

4. Encourage varied solutions, and point out the validity of each. Few interesting problems have only one method of solution. Children become better problem solvers if they can see and compare different strategies for solving the same problem. They may then be more likely to try another approach if a given one doesn't work.

5. *Encourage manipulation of materials, or in a more general sense, of ideas.* Children should develop confidence to try out new techniques and new combinations of ideas. Manipulative embodiments of ideas are especially appropriate for encouraging children to take intellectual risks and to experiment.

Finding Similarities Among Challenges

Certain problems appear in different guises in several different challenge sets. This indicates how the structure of a given problem can fit in many different contexts. Most of the challenges in this collection can and should be adapted and, when possible, phrased in terms of the students' immediate environment and interests. When students see and recognize the same structure arising in different places they may appreciate the power of the abstract thinking characteristic of mathematics – that a solution strategy for one problem can be applied to another problem.

One challenge that has been used in this way is a classic. In the commentaries it is referred to as the "cows and chickens" problem. An example is:

> *A pen on a farm contained only cows and chickens. I looked over the top of the fence and I saw 10 heads. I looked under the fence and I saw 32 feet. How many cows were there?*

This is a nice challenge to discuss with a diverse group of children, because many different strategies will be attempted, some of which are described below.

Some children may use a *guess and check* strategy, where they try out a certain number of cows, and see if it works. For example, if there were 5 cows (with 20 legs), then there would be 5 chickens (with 10 legs), making a total of 30 legs. This total is close to 32, so they might next try a nearby number.

Students may combine this strategy with one of *manipulating models*. Younger children may find it easier to think about the problem if they have a number of little cards with pictures of cows or chickens. Other students may produce their own models by *drawing a picture*.

Students who use the *guess and check* strategy may organize their work and *make a table*, such as the one below.

number of cows	number of chickens	number of legs
1	9	22
2	8	24
3	7	26
⋮	⋮	⋮

Such a table can help students to verify the accuracy of their results, and may lead them *to look for a pattern* – for example, as an extra cow is added, a chicken is subtracted, and the number of legs increases by 2. Counting on by this pattern, it is seen that if there are 6 cows, there are 4 chickens and the number of legs is 32.

The above strategies may be successful when there are not too many choices, but if the numbers of cows, chickens, and legs were larger, it might help to look at extremes to get an idea of where to start. That is, suppose that all the animals were cows – then there would be 40 legs. If all were chickens, there would be 20 legs. The fact that there are 32 legs suggests testing a situation where a little more than half the animals are cows.

Children have been known to use *reasoning* as follows: Think of the cows as standing on just two legs, with two held up in the air (admittedly, a difficult feat for a cow!). Then 20 legs are on the ground (because there are 10 animals), and since there are 32 legs in all, and 32 – 20 = 12, then 12 legs must be held up in the air, 2 for each cow. So there must be 6 cows.

Finally, older students may use *algebra* to approach the problem. If C is the number of cows, then (10 – C) is the number of chickens. The number of cow legs is 4C, and the number of chicken legs is 2(10 – C). One can then set up and solve the equation:

$$4C + 2(10 - C) = 32.$$

Children will become better problem solvers if they are aware that they can tackle a new problem by selecting one or more from a variety of strategies. Sometimes one strategy works better than others, but usually there is more than one possible strategy for solving a problem.

Using the Challenge Sets with Teachers

Some of the challenge sets are especially useful for preservice teachers, by giving them a sense of how mathematics topics develop over the grades, and also providing some experience with non-routine problem solving (which is often lacking in their own educational experiences). The challenge sets have been used in inservice courses with groups of teachers of varied grade levels, and have provided a focus for discussion of how mathematics content and methods grow and change through a child's school experience.

To empower teachers to select and develop challenges appropriate for their own students, the in-service teacher trainer can cut up the challenges with letters removed, and mount them on file cards. Teachers can be given a stack – possibly all eight, or possible fewer depending on the range of grade levels involved – and asked first to solve them, and then to sequence them in order of difficulty. Finally, the teachers can be asked to select a couple for their own classes, and to come up with a similar challenge of their own. Once they have tried some of the sets related to manipulatives or themes, they can be given a new manipulative or theme, and asked to come up with new challenges. Challenge Set: 11, A Bag of Nuts, was developed in this way, where groups of teachers were presented with an unopened bag of mixed nuts.

References

Azzolino, Solvey and Hughes, ed. *Mathematics and Humor*. (NCTM, 1978)

Banwell, Saunders, and Tahta. *Starting Points*, (Tarquin Publications, 1986)

Barrata-Lorton, Mary. *Mathematics Their Way*. (Addison-Wesley, 1976)

Barson, Alan. *Geoboard Activity Cards*. (Scott Resources, 1971)

Beyer, Jinny. *Patchwork Patterns*. (EPM Publications, Inc., 1979)

Bolt, Brian. *The Amazing Mathematical Amusement Arcade*. (Cambridge University Press, 1982)

Burns, Marilyn. *The I Hate Mathematics! Book*. (Little, Brown and Co., 1975)

Burns, Marilyn. *A Collection of Math Lessons From Grades 3 Through 6*. (The Math Solution Publications, 1987)

Burns, Marilyn. *Math for Smarty Pants*. (Little, Brown and Co., 1982)

Burns, Marilyn and Tank, Bonnie. *A Collection of Math Lessons From Grades 1 Through 3*. (The Math Solution Publications, 1987)

Charles, Lester and O'Daffer. *How to Evaluate Progress in Problem Solving*. (NCTM, 1987)

Comprehensive School Mathematics Program. *CSMP in Action*. (CEMREL, 1978)

Creative Publications. *Cooperative Problem Solving Using Tangrams*. (Creative Publications, 1989)

Cuisenaire Company of America. *"Learning With ..."* booklets which accompany manipulatives. (Cuisenaire, 1991)

Dahl, Roald. *Matilda*. (Viking Penguin, 1988)

Dahl, Roald. *The Witches*. (Farrar Straus Giroux, 1983)

Davis, Robert. *Discovery in Mathematics*. (Addison-Wesley, 1964)

Davis, Robert. *Explorations in Mathematics*. (Addison-Wesley, 1967)

Dudeney, Henry Ernest. *536 Puzzles and Curious Problems*. (Scribner's, 1967)

Fuys, David and Tischler, Rosamond Welchman. *Teaching Mathematics in the Elementary School*. (Little, Brown and Co., 1979)

Gutcheon, Beth. *The Perfect Patchwork Primer*. (Penguin, 1973)

Hill, Jane M., Ed. *Geometry for Grades K-6, Readings from the Arithmetic Teacher*. (NCTM, 1987)

Institute for the Development of Educational Alternatives, Inc. *Provoking Thoughts, The Magazine Devoted to the Thinker in All of Us*. Published bi-monthly by I.D.E.A., P.O. Box 1004, Austin, MN 55912.

Kamii, Constance and Devries, Rheta. *Group Games in Early Education, Implications of Piaget's Theory*. (NAEYC, 1980)

Mathis, Sharon Bell. *The Hundred Penny Box*. (Puffin, 1986)

Myllar, Rolf. *How Big Is a Foot?* (Atheneum, 1962)

National Council of Teachers of Mathematics. *Curriculum and Evaluation Standards for School Mathematics*. (NCTM, 1988)

National Council of Teachers of Mathematics. *Professional Standards for Teaching Mathematics*. (NCTM, 1991)

National Council of Teachers of Mathematics. *Estimation and Mental Computation, 1986 Yearbook*. Ed. Harold L. Schoen. (NCTM, 1986)

O'Brien, Thomas. *Wollygoggles and Other Creatures*. (Cuisenaire, 1980)

Pittman, Helena Claire. *A Grain of Rice*. (Hastings House, 1986)

Read, R.C. *Tangrams – 330 Puzzles*. (Dover, 1965)

Sawyer, W. W. *Vision in Elementary Mathematics*. (Penguin, 1964)

Schwartz, David M. and Kellogg, Steven. *How Much Is a Million?* (Lothrop, Lee and Shepard, 1985)

Simon, Seymour. *The Optical Illusion Book*. (William Morrow and Co., 1984)

Slobodkina, Esther. *Caps for Sale*. (Scholastic, 1984)

Trivett, John. *Introducing Geoboards*. (Cuisenaire, 1973, 1983)

Unified Science and Mathematics for Elementary School. *Dice Design*. (EDC, 1974)

Welchman-Tischler, Rosamond. *How to Use Children's Literature to Teach Mathematics*. (NCTM, 1992)

Wells, David. *Can You Solve These?* (Tarquin Publications, 1982)

CHALLENGE SET : 1

cuisenaire rods

These challenges are about Cuisenaire rods. These colored rods have a square centimeter base, and come in lengths of 1 to 10 centimeters. Their colors are often indicated by letters as shown.

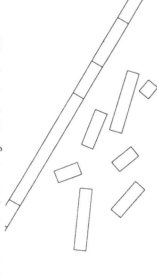

C. A Long Train

If all of the rods in one set were placed end to end in a train, how long would the train be?

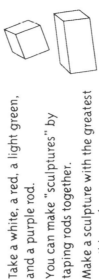

F. Squares

Can you make a square using exactly one of each rod?

Can you make a square using exactly two of each rod? three? four?

A. Trains of the Same Length

In how many different ways can you make a train as long as a yellow rod?

Here are three different ways to make such a train:

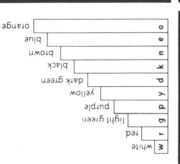

D. Inequalities

How many solutions are there?

(The same or different rods can go in the □ and the △.)

G. Sculptures

Take a white, a red, a light green, and a purple rod.

You can make "sculptures" by taping rods together.

Make a sculpture with the greatest possible surface area.

Make one with the least possible surface area.

B. Addition Sentences

Use just these rods: r, r, g, g, p, y.

In how many ways can you make addition sentences with them?

Here are some examples.

r + r = p   r + y = g + p

E. Measuring the Cat

I measured my cat (head to tip of tail) with red rods and they fit exactly.

I measured with blue rods and they also fit exactly.

When I tried with purple rods, they didn't fit. Then the cat ran away.

How long is the cat?

H. Clues

I am longer than a yellow rod.

No rod has half of my length.

There is a rod with one third of my length.

Who am I?

Can any clue be omitted?

Commentary:1 CUISENAIRE RODS

Cuisenaire rods are an attractive and versatile tool for developing mathematical thinking. In primary grades, rods are often used to develop the interpretation of addition as putting lengths together, leading eventually to understanding of the number line as a model for arithmetic. In upper grades, they are useful as a model for fractions. At all levels they are helpful in learning about metric units of length, area and volume, because the square base measures 1 cm on a side. Finally, they invite play, which is likely to involve spatial concepts.

The lengths are color-coded, and students who will work extensively with rods should learn this code. Note that the code corresponds to the first letter of most colors (white, red, light green, purple, yellow, dark green, orange), but for the 3 colors beginning with 'b', the last letters are used (brown, black, blue). A nice challenge might be to have students figure out why the code is formed in this way. Some teachers have students memorize the number equivalents of the colors, however, others feel that this practice reduces the potential of the rods for later work with fractions and algebraic concepts.

A
This can be done just by experimenting. A nice pattern emerges if you consider how many ways each length can be made. The length of a white rod can be made in just 1 way, the white itself. A red rod can be made in 2 ways (how?), and a light green in 4 ways (how?). At this point you might see the pattern of doubling, and suspect that the purple can be made in 8 ways. Add all of these ways to make lengths less than a yellow together and you get 1+2+4+8 = 15. (This happens to be 1 less than 16, the number of ways to make the length of a yellow. Could this be coincidence? (See Calenders, Set 34, Challenge H.)

B
There are many solutions. To find them all, students need a systematic way to classify sentences that they find. You might ask students to write each solution on a separate slip of paper, and then to arrange them. They might sort them by how many rods are used. There are only six 3-rod combinations, (r + r = p, r + g = y, g + r = y, and their 'reverses' p = r + r, y = r + g, y = g + r). The 4-rod combination r, g, p and y yields 8 sentences (r + y = g + p, y + r = g + p, r + y = p + g and y + r = p + g, and their 'reverses'). The 4-rod combination r, r, g, g yields 4 more (r + g = r + g, r + g = g + r, g + r = r + g, g + r = g + r, and their 'reverses'). No addition sentence can be made using all 6 rods (because the sum of their lengths is odd). To make a 5-rod sentence, you need to leave out one of the odd-length rods, g or y. The combination p + g = g + r + r leads to 12 sentences by rearranging terms, and the combination y + g = r + r + p leads to 12 more. That makes a total of 46 sentences, a large number for students to find.

C
Students might check the listing on the side of a set's container, and calculate accordingly. You might leave the challenge as an estimate, and just show a random assortment of rods in a clear container. To check on their estimates, students might sort rods by color, then count and multiply for each color (i.e. 5 blacks gives 5x7 cm, or 35 cm).

D
This can be approached in a systematic way, as in challenge B. If the sum □ + △ is less than y, then it must be equal to w, r, g, or p. Find the pattern of how many solutions there are to each of the equations □ + △ = w (0 solutions). □ + △ = r (1 solution). □ + △ = g (2 solutions). □ + △ = p (3 solutions), □ + △ = y (4 solutions). Add to get the total, 10. The problem can also be solved by simply listing all possible inequalities.

E
Red rods measure 2 cm, blue measure 9 cm, and purple measure 4 cm. The cat's length is a common multiple of 2 and 9, but not a multiple of 4. Thus the cat could be 18 cm, 54 cm or 90 cm, but not 36 cm or 72 cm. Cats are never as long as 90 cm, and a cat old enough to run away is longer than 18 cm. The cat is 54 cm long.

F
Solid squares cannot be made with any of these combinations of lengths, because the first is equivalent to 55 whites, the second to 110, the third to 165, and the fourth to 220 whites, none of which is a square number. To make a "hollow square" or just the outline, the total number of whites must be a multiple of 4, and so only the fourth is possible.

G
It may help to restrict this problem and say that rods must touch in regions which are multiples of square centimeters, or cm². Note that the original surface areas of the rods in cm² are 6 (w), 10 (r), 14 (g) and 18 (p) — a pattern which totals 48 cm². When two rods are glued together, the surface area diminishes by twice the area of contact. To make a sculpture with the least surface area, glue the rods together so that they touch as much as possible. In the arrangement here, they touch along 7 cm², and so the surface area is 48 – (2 x 7) = 34 cm² (which you can also compute directly). To make the greatest possible surface area, glue the rods so that each only touches its neighbor on 1 cm². One way to do this is to join the rods into one long rod which has surface area 48 – (2 x 3) = 42 cm². (Note: rubber cement wipes off easily.)

H
Blue. The first clue says the rod is d, k, n, or o. The second says the rod is w, g, y, k or e. The third says the rod is g, d or e. No clue can be omitted because each pair of clues leads to two possible answers. Students can make up their own sets of clues. See *Hidden Rods, Hidden Numbers* by M. Charbonneau for more examples.

CHALLENGE SET : 2

pattern blocks

These challenges all refer to Pattern Blocks, which are made in the following colors and shapes:

yellow   red   blue   green   orange   tan

To work on the problems, you should have several of each color.

C. Green, Blue and Yellow

I covered 6 yellow blocks with green and blue blocks.

I used 28 green and blue blocks.

How many green blocks did I use?

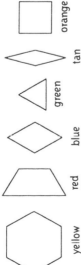

F. Symmetry

Take 3 each of the yellow, red, blue and green pieces.

Use the 12 blocks to fill in equilateral triangles with patterns that have:

- line but not rotational symmetry
- rotational but not line symmetry
- both line and rotational symmetry

Draw your results.

A. Different Ways.

In how many different ways can you cover the yellow hexagon with other blocks?

D. Covering the Page

How many green pieces would it take to cover a piece of paper the size of this one?

How many red pieces?

G. Angles

Take one of each color piece.
Use these 6 pieces to fill a polygonal region.
Draw your polygon.

Find the measure of each angle of your polygon. Use only the blocks.

Find the sum of the measures of the angles of your polygon.

B. Tiling Patterns

Take some red pieces and some blue pieces. Make a pattern so that there is no space, and you could continue it indefinitely.

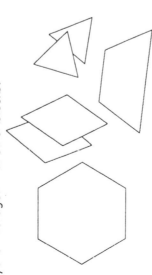

E. A Large Hexagon

Fill in a hexagonal region using 8 pieces of any colors.

How many green pieces cover it?

What is the largest hexagonal region you could make with 8 pieces?

What is the smallest?

H. Comparing Areas

Which has greater area, a blue diamond or a square? Why?

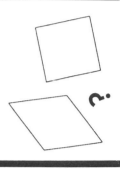

What fraction of the area of the square is the area of the tan diamond? Why?

Commentary:2
PATTERN BLOCKS

Pattern Blocks are appealing and rich in mathematical possibilities. Students may record their work on triangular grid paper, or with templates cut to the exact size of the blocks, or by gluing colored paper cut-outs of the blocks. They can also record a pattern by pressing a piece of self-adhesive plastic on it, and using this to lift the blocks onto a photocopy machine.

A Children will discover that to cover the yellow hexagon, only red, blue and green blocks are suitable. To answer this challenge, children must first decide what "different" means. For example, are the following pairs "different?"

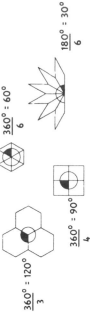

Let us consider two coverings the "same" if one can be rotated to get the other. Then results are as follows. Note that it helps to have a system for counting. Here it is done by the largest block in the arrangement:

largest block	number of ways
yellow	1
red	4
blue	4
green	1
total =	10

B Here are three of the many possible solutions. If children record their solutions by gluing cut-out construction paper shapes, or by using rubber stamps in the two shapes, their results can be categorized. Which patterns are built in strips? Which radiate from the center? Which use the same number of reds as blues?

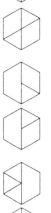

C This is a variant of the "cows and chickens" problem described in the Introduction. The many possible solution strategies include trial and error, and making a chart and noting a pattern. Children might reason as follows. If all 6 yellows were covered with blues, it would take 18 blocks, which is 10 too few. Replacing 1 blue by 2 greens adds 1 block to the total, and so 10 blues should be replaced, leaving 8 blues and 20 greens.

D One way to solve this is to note that the green triangle has sides of one inch, and so 11 fit across the long side. A second row of 12 will fill in and make a strip about 7/8 inch wide. It will take 10 of these strips to cover the page, making a total of 230 blocks. (This solution assumes that blocks cannot be cut, so that a little more than the page is actually covered.)

E There are many ways to make hexagons with 8 blocks. The one on the left below has the least area, being covered by 8 green blocks. (Note that the triangle has less area than the tan diamond — see Challenge H — and so the middle hexagon has greater area.) The one on the right requires 32 green blocks to cover it, the largest possible area.

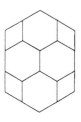

F Here are sample solutions to the first two challenges. The third is impossible.

G This is an open question, with many possible solutions. Here is a polygon with 8 sides made from one of each block. Other solutions may have more than 8 sides. Students can use the blocks alone to find angle measures of each piece, by arranging identical corners around a point.

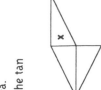

$$\frac{360^\circ}{3} = 120^\circ \qquad \frac{360^\circ}{4} = 90^\circ$$

$$\frac{360^\circ}{6} = 60^\circ \qquad \frac{180^\circ}{6} = 30^\circ$$

This works for all angles but the obtuse one on the tan block, which is seen to be the sum of the angle of a yellow and the acute angle of a tan, or $120^\circ + 30^\circ = 150^\circ$. Have students share their data, including the number of sides of the polygon and the sum of the angle measures. They may see a pattern:

number of sides	sum of angle measures
8	1080°
9	1260°
10	1440°
⋮	⋮

Successive entries differ by 180°, leading to the formula: the sum of the angle measures of a polygon with n sides is $(n - 2) \times 180^\circ$.

H Students can compare the orange and blue blocks visually. If the blue is placed over the orange as shown, it is seen that the "extra" part of the blue could cover only the dotted part of the orange, and so a narrow strip on the top of the orange would be uncovered. Thus the orange has greater area. To compare orange and tan blocks, imagine the tan superimposed on the green as shown. The line segment marked "x" has one half the length of the triangle's side, or 1/2 inch. Thus, the tan parallelogram has area base x height, or $1 \times 1/2 = 1/2$. This is exactly half of the area of the square.

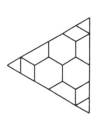

CHALLENGE SET : 3

geoboards

Try these challenges on a geoboard, a square array of pegs over which you can stretch rubber bands. You can make a geoboard from a square piece of wood and nails (preferably with rounded heads). To get exact placement of nails, place a piece of graph paper over the wood, hammer nails through it, then tear off the paper. The challenges are stated in terms of 5x5 geoboards, but most can be adapted to other sizes.

A. Squares

This square has 12 boundary pegs and 4 interior pegs.

Make a square with 4 boundary pegs and 1 interior peg.

What other squares can you make?

B. How Would It Look?

Make this shape as it would look from the other side, if you were looking through a transparent geoboard.

C. Words and Polygons

The 6-letter word CHARMS makes a 6-sided polygon on this geoboard.

Can you find a 3-letter word that makes a polygon? a 4-letter word? a 5-letter word? a word with more than 6 letters?

A· B· C· D· E·
F· G· H· I· J·
K· L· M· N· O·
P· Q· R· S· T·
U· V· W· X· Y·

D. Changes

Change this figure to make one with:

• same area, greater perimeter
• same area, lesser perimeter
• same perimeter, greater area
• same perimeter, lesser area

E. Clues

I have a right angle and two acute angles.

I have 4 sides.

My area is 3 square units.

I have no interior pegs.

What could I be?

Draw me on geoboard paper.

F. Triangles

One side of this triangle has unit length.

unit length

How many different triangles which have one side of unit length can be made on a geoboard?

G. Half of a Rectangle

In how many ways can you place one rubber band on this geoboard figure to cut it in half?

H. Area

Make four different shapes that have an area of 4 square units.

Find the perimeter of each.

What is the maximum possible perimeter for a shape with area 4?

What is the minimum possible perimeter?

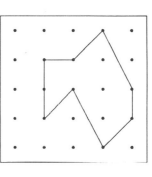

The Mathematical Toolbox   © 1992 Cuisenaire Company of America, Inc.

Commentary: 3
GEOBOARDS

Geoboards are appealing to students of a wide range of ages. Young children are able to create and display forms which they might not be able to represent otherwise, owing to limitations in their manual dexterity. The structure of the pegs on a geoboard limits what geometric forms can be made, but provides a context for many interesting problems related to measurement for older students. If each student has his or her own geoboard, you can ask each to make a shape and then display it to the class. You can then use various formats presented in other challenge sets — for example, Which One is Different?, Set 14, or Concept Cards, Set 13. For each of these, you can display some of the students' creations on geoboards in front of the class. (The videotape "Mathematics with Manipulatives: Geoboards," available from Cuisenaire Co., shows how many geometric concepts arise in such an activity in a lesson taught by Marilyn Burns.)

When you present any of the challenges to students, provide sheets of dot paper so that students can record their explorations.

A Have students articulate what boundary pegs and interior pegs are (i.e., boundary pegs are those which are actually touched by the rubber band, and interior pegs are those which are inside the rubber band but not touched). Students should also decide what squares are "different." Perhaps they will decide that two squares which are congruent (have the same shape and size) will be considered the same. You might give a hint that the sides do not have to be horizontal or vertical. To the right are drawn all 8 possible different sizes of squares on a 5 x 5 board.

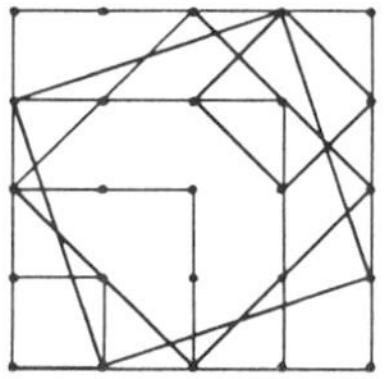

B If you have a transparent geoboard, it is easy to check solutions to this challenge by actually turning it over and placing it on top of a geoboard. You can also draw the shape on a sheet of acetate.

C This connection between the geometric framework of the geoboard and letters leads to a lot of interesting challenges. Encourage children to discover that not all 3-letter words make polygons (for example, JOY does not). The 4-letter words SING and TERM don't make polygons, but TERN does. Children might want to make their initials on the geoboard. (If any are called "Zachary," you could use the "Y" peg for both "Y" and "Z.")

D Here are some possible solutions. Students should be challenged to find solutions which require the least possible changes from the given figure.

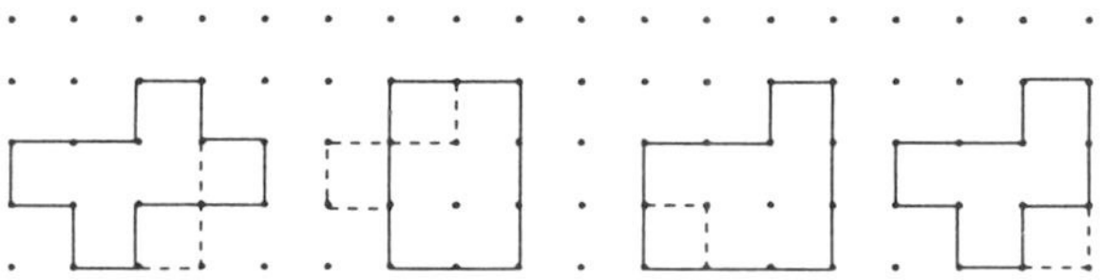

E Here is a solution. There are probably others. After students have tried one of these, have them make up a set of clues for their own creations.

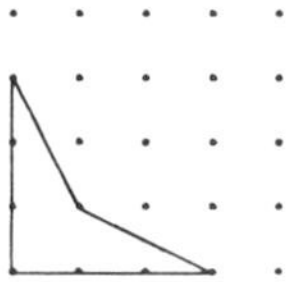

F As in Challenge A, students will need to refine this question — when are two triangles considered "different?" Here is a way to think about the problem if two triangles are considered congruent when they are congruent. All such triangles would be congruent to one with the side of unit length horizontal in the lower left corner of the geoboard, that is, with U and V as two of the vertices (using the lettering of Challenge C). Consider what pegs could be the third vertex. Any peg from A to T would serve as a third vertex of the triangle. However there are some

A·	B·	C·	D·	E·
F·	G·	H·	I·	J·
K·	L·	M·	N·	O·
P·	Q·	R·	S·	T·
U·	V·	W·	X·	Y·

duplications — AUV is congruent to BUV, FUV to GUV, KUV to LUV and PUV to QUV. All others are different. Thus there are 16 different congruent triangles, corresponding to these 16 dots: B, C, D, E, G, H, I, J, L, M, N, O, Q, R, S, and T.

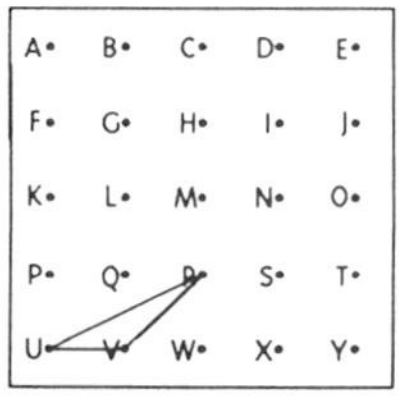

G Three of the many solutions are shown. Again students should refine the question — are they looking for ways to make two congruent regions (a–c below), or two regions with the same area (d–e)?

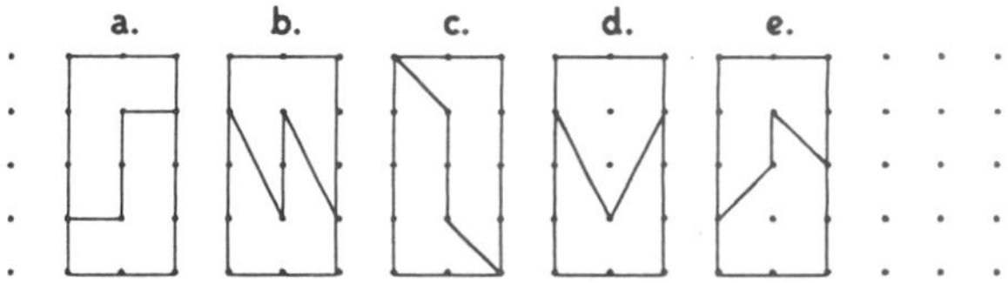

a.   b.   c.   d.   e.

H This is a suitable challenge for students who have learned about the Pythagorean Theorem. For some shapes, they may want to find the perimeter using a calculator. Below are two possible candidates for minimum perimeter. Students might contrast various techniques for finding which has smaller perimeter: direct measurement, use of a calculator, or arithmetic operations on the numerical expressions. Here is a "shorthand" summary of an argument that A has greater perimeter.

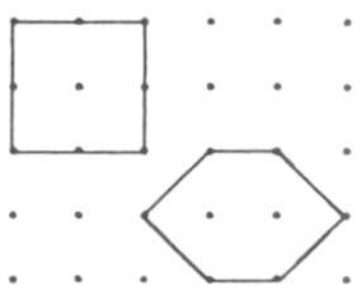

Perimeter of A = 8
Perimeter of B = $4\sqrt{2} + 2$
Which is greater?

Asking   8   (?) $4\sqrt{2} + 2$ is equivalent to asking

     6   (?) $4\sqrt{2}$

or   6/4   (?) $\sqrt{2}$

or   3/2   (?) $\sqrt{2}$

or $(3/2)^2$ (?) $(\sqrt{2})^2$

or   9/4   (?)   2.

Since 9/4 > 2, A has greater perimeter.

Further ideas for the use of geoboards are found in *Geoboard Activity Cards* (Primary or Intermediate sets) by Alan Barson, and *Introducing Geoboards* by John Trivett.

CHALLENGE SET : 4

tangrams

Try these challenges with a set of Tangram pieces. This classic puzzle is made from a square (usually 10 cm on a side) divided into seven parts as shown.

Many interesting and life-like shapes can be made with these seven pieces. Play around with them. What can you make?

A. What Shapes?

Take the two small triangles.

What can you make from them?

Can you make a ▢ ?

a ◺ ? a ▱ ?

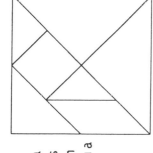

B. Tangram Clues

Here are some clues about a shape.

The shape is made from 3 pieces.

The shape has 4 sides.

One of the pieces is not a triangle.

Two of the pieces are just the same.

What could the shape be?

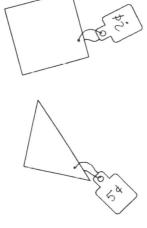

C. Buying Tangram Pieces

Suppose that the small triangle costs 5¢.

How much will each of the other pieces cost?

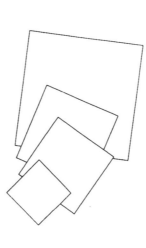

D. Making Squares

Can you make a square with 1 piece? with 2 pieces? with 3? with 4? 5? 6? 7?

E. What Percent?

All seven Tangram pieces make up a square.

What percent of the area of the square is made up of triangles?

F. Your Initials

Make one of your initials with all seven pieces.

Describe your shape. (For example: How many sides does it have? Are there parallel sides? What types of angles are there?)

G. Paperfolding

Take a square piece of paper.

How can you fold the paper to make a complete set of Tangram pieces?

(As a challenge, start with an irregular piece of paper with ragged edges.)

H. A Famous Theorem

From 2 sets of Tangrams, take 2 large triangles, 2 middle triangles, and 4 small triangles.

Trace around a middle triangle on paper.

What famous theorem of geometry can you illustrate by arranging all 8 triangles around this shape?

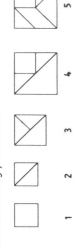

Children of all ages enjoy Tangram puzzles which challenge them to use the seven pieces to duplicate a shape or to cover a printed outline exactly. It is amazing how many pictures can be made with these seven pieces. Below are shown a few samples of the many puzzles found in *Tangrams, 330 Puzzles* by R.C. Read.

(You may have seen puzzles like these using other shapes. You or your students can construct similar puzzles by tracing around patterns made with other shapes in the classroom, such as pattern blocks.) Teachers are sometimes surprised by the spatial abilities demonstrated by students when solving these puzzles. Students who excel at such spatial tasks may not be skillful in other areas of mathematics, such as computation. Classroom experience with Tangram puzzles can be a welcome image-booster for such students.

The seven Tangram pieces are especially attractive as a teaching material because there are many teachers' guides for how to use Tangrams to teach specific mathematics topics (for example, *Tangram Treasury* by Jan Fair). The fact that all pieces can be covered with some number of the small triangles means that the Tangram pieces are useful for developing concepts of area and fractions. The challenges below suggest the range of mathematics topics that can be approached through Tangrams. Each can be adapted to suit many different levels of difficulty.

A If the triangles must fit exactly along edges, just the three shapes shown are possible. However without this restriction, many more shapes can

be made. The challenge can be extended to making shapes from 3 or 4 of the pieces. Students can add their creations to a display on a bulletin board.

B Four possible solutions are shown below.

This type of puzzle is easy for students to make up. There may be many solutions.

The book *Cooperative Problem Solving Using Tangrams* (Creative Publications, 1989) has an interesting way to use puzzles such as these. For a group of four children, write each of four clues on a separate card. Each child gets a set of Tangram pieces and a card, and only that child can look at the card. Children take turns reading their cards aloud to the group, and as they do this, each child tries to construct a shape which satisfies all four clues. They must listen carefully to each other, and put the different pieces of information together. Finally, they compare solutions. As an additional challenge, each child should try to find a different solution.

C Students should describe the assumptions they make when answering this. Most will assume that a piece with double the area of another should be double the price. The middle-sized triangle, the square, and the parallelogram all have twice the area of the small triangle, and so each would cost 2 × 5¢, or 10¢. The large triangle has four times the area of the small triangle, and so each would cost 4 × 5¢ or 20¢. You could ask the "price" of regions which can be covered by various numbers of small triangles. Vary the price of the small triangle to practice different multiplication tables.

D Below is shown how to make squares using 1–5 pieces, and the 7-piece solution is shown on the student page. If you allow two sets to be used, a square can be made with 6 pieces. (For example, you can

---

take the solution shown for a square made with 5 pieces, and replace the square by two small triangles.) This cannot be done using just one set.

1   2   3   4   5

E Students should see that all pieces are made up of 1, 2 or 4 of the small triangles, and that there are 16 small triangles in the whole square. The triangles in the set can be covered with 12 small triangles, and so occupy 12/16 or 75% of the area. Similar questions can also be phrased in terms of fractional parts. For example, "What fraction of the area of the whole square is the small square piece?" (2/16 = 1/8)

F This one has many answers. Have students share their descriptions verbally and see if other students can construct the initial in the same way using only the descriptions. You can remove the requirement that all seven pieces be used to make the initial, and then ask for the area of the letter using the small triangle as a unit.

G If students experiment with folding paper, they find that it is in fact easy to form a right angle by making one fold, and then folding the fold line on itself. If you ask students to describe their techniques for folding to get a Tangram set verbally, they will be drawn to use a rich geometric vocabulary — for example, angles, diagonals, midpoints, parallel lines, ... This approach is described in *Geometry for Grades K–6, Readings from the Arithmetic Teacher*, ed. Jane M. Hill (NCTM, 1987), pages 133–137.

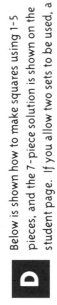

H This is the Pythagorean Theorem. The area of the square built on the hypotenuse of the middle triangle is equal to the sum of the areas of the squares built on the other two sides.

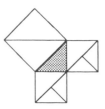
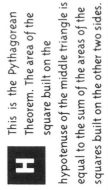

CHALLENGE SET : 5

two-color counters

To work on these challenges use two-color counters, such as the plastic commercially available ones, which are red on one side and yellow on the other. You can also use a home-made substitute such as squares of cardboard, bottle caps, pennies, or dried lima beans that have been spray-painted on one side.

Note: ● represents red and ○ yellow.

A. A Pattern

Here is a pattern of counters.

If you make this pattern and continue it until you have 10 yellow counters in a row and then stop, how many of each color will you need?

B. Four Counters

In how many different ways can you fill these four spaces with four counters of the two colors?

Counters can be the same or different colors. Put one in each box, for example:

○	●	○	●

C. A Puzzle

There are twice as many red counters as yellow counters.

There are twelve more reds than yellows.

How many counters are there?

D. Shopping

Suppose that red counters cost 18¢ and yellow counters cost 14¢. You bought 12 counters and were charged exactly $2.00.

How many of each color did you buy?

E. Fraction Flip

I had some counters. One-half of them were red.

I flipped over two of them, and then one-third of them were red.

How many counters did I have?

F. What Is the Rule?

In this arrangement of counters, each row is determined by the row above.

What will be in the next row?

? ? ? ? ?

G. Rows of Counters

How can you arrange 5 red counters and 5 yellow counters in 5 rows, where each row has 2 chips of each color?

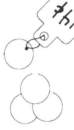

H. A Pattern Again

In this pattern, what will be the color of the 100th counter?

○○○○○●○○○○○○●○○○○ ...

The Mathematical Toolbox   © 1992 Cuisenaire Company of America, Inc.

These challenges illustrate how an extremely simple material can be used as a tool for thinking about a variety of mathematical problems. If you do not have the red and yellow counters available, try to make some alternative available to all students. It is easy to spray paint a bag of dried lima beans, or find some cardboard that is a different color on each side and cut it into squares on a paper cutter. Some challenges do not require the counters to be two-sided — simply use two different types of counters.

A Chapter 1 in the book *A Collection of Math Lessons From Grades 1 Through 3* by Marilyn Burns and Bonnie Tank illustrates how this challenge can be the basis for a first grade lesson rich in mathematical exploration and communication. There are many ways in which children might find the sum of $1 + 1 + 2 + 1 + 3 + 1 + 4 + \ldots + 10$. Some will draw all of the chips and count them. Others might first recognize that there will be 10 red chips, and then $1 + 2 + 3 + \ldots + 10$ yellow ones. A very sophisticated approach is to group this sum into 10's: $(1 + 9) + (2 + 8) + (3 + 7) + (4 + 6) + 5 + 10$, a total of 5 tens and 5 for the yellows, and so 65 in all.

B Children who try to find all of the different arrangements without any particular system are likely to miss some. It is easier to be sure that all are found if children use some system — for example, first find 1 with all yellow (oooo), then 4 with just one red (●ooo, o●oo, oo●o, ooo●), then 6 with two reds (●●oo, ●o●o, ●oo●, o●●o, o●o●, oo●●), then 4 with three reds and finally 1 with four reds — a total of 16. Children might notice that the number of arrangements with one red is the same as the number of arrangements with one yellow, etc. As an extension, try this problem with 2 chips, 3, 5, etc. and look for a pattern. An approach to this problem for older children is described in Coins, Set 8, Challenge F.

C Students might arrive at the answer to this one by trial and error. They might also analyze the situation, and realize that if there are twice as many reds as yellows and 12 more reds than yellows, there must be 12 yellows, and so 36 counters. Students might try making up more problems of this type.

D This problem is an example of the "cows and chickens" problem described in the Introduction, and appears in other disguises in other challenge sets. There are many strategies for it. Sometimes students use trial and error. They may organize their results in a table and notice a pattern. Some may try the extreme cases. Suppose that all 12 chips purchased were red, then they would cost $12 \times \$.18 = \$2.16$ which is 16¢ too much. Since each red costs 4¢ more than a yellow, the required charge will be obtained if 4 reds are replaced with yellows, that is, 8 reds and 4 yellow were bought. Encourage students to make up more challenges like this, and also try some with no solution. For example, if $2.02 was the charge for 12 chips, there would be no solution.

E As in challenge C, this one might be solved by trial and error. A way to analyze the situation is as follows: when 2 counters were flipped, the fraction that were red changed from one-half to one-third, a difference of one-sixth. This means that one-sixth of the original number was 2, so there were 12 counters at the start.

F Students might be offered a hint by drawing lines from each counter to the two above.

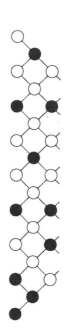

Then it is seen that two of the same color yield a red, two of different colors yield a yellow. A hint might be to think of reds and yellows as odds and evens, with the chip representing the sum of the two chips above.

investigate is how to start such an array so that eventually all the counters in a row are red.

This pattern represents a very simple model for population growth. Think of the yellow counters representing presence of life, and reds its absence. When organisms are too closely crowded or too far apart, they cannot reproduce, corresponding to the rule that two of the same color yield a red. Organisms can only reproduce if there are some but not too many of each color, a combination of red and yellow.

G A solution is the five-pointed star shown. To help find this, think that there are only 10 counters. Five rows with 4 in each row requires 20 counters, unless some are in more than one row.

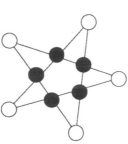

H Students might approach this by actually drawing 100 counters. Encourage them to see patterns. The triangular numbers, 1, 3, 6, 10, ... are mentioned in Cubes, Set 6, Challenges A and E. Red chips occur in the positions 1, 3, 6, 10, ... It appears that red counters occupy positions of triangular numbers. Since the 13th and 14th triangular numbers are 91 and 105, the 100th chip will be yellow. (If you want to convince yourself that the reds really do fall in the positions of triangular numbers, consider that they are in positions $1, 2 + \underline{1}, 3 + \underline{3}, 4 + \underline{6}, 5 + \underline{10}, \ldots$. The last is explained by there being 5 red counters so far, and $1 + 2 + 3 + 4 = 10$ yellow ones. Notice that the underlined numbers are the triangular numbers, and the numbers being added to them are just what is needed to generate the next triangular number.)

CHALLENGE SET : 6

cubes

These challenges are to be done with cubes — wooden ones or interlocking plastic ones (such as Snap Cubes, Unifix, Multilink, or centicubes). Sugar cubes would also work (as long as they are the small, cubical ones.) Challenge H requires a cube which measures 1 centimeter on each edge (a centicube). A standard die would be helpful in Challenge D.

F. Views of a Building

Can you make a "building" out of cubes that has these side, front and top views?

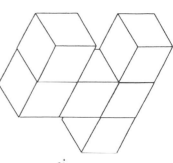

SIDE   **FRONT**   **TOP**

Can you do it a different way?

G. A Painted Cube

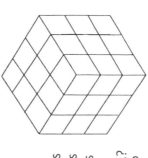

Suppose the entire surface of this cube (including the bottom) has been painted. If it is cut into smaller cubes as shown, how many cubes will have: 0 faces painted? 1 face painted? 2? 3? 4? more than 4?

H. Surface Area of a Sculpture

Use six centicubes to make a "sculpture." Cubes can be "glued" only along an entire face. Can you make such a sculpture that has:

a. volume of 6 cm³, a surface area 22 cm²?

b. volume of 6 cm³, a surface area 21 cm²?

C. Patterns of Five

Arrange five cubes on the grid paper so that each cube rests on the paper, and touches another cube along a face.

How many different arrangements like this can you make?

D. Pictures of Dice

Which of the pictures above could be a view of a standard die, made from a pattern like this?

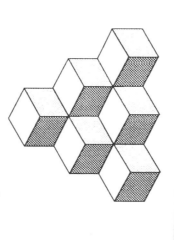

E. Building a Staircase

How many cubes does i· take to build a staircase, 3 cubes wide, that has 10 steps?

How many cubes would it take to build a staircase this size, if the cubes used are half as wide as the original cubes?

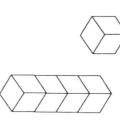

A. Building With Cubes

How many cubes does it take to build this?

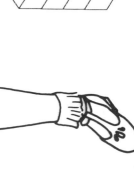

B. Measuring With Cubes

Estimate how many cubes it would take to make a train as tall as you are.

The Mathematical Toolbox
© 1992 Cuisenaire Company of America, Inc.

Cubes are a natural material to count, especially in contexts where patterns arise, as in Challenges A, E or G. They make good units of measurement (standard or non-standard, depending on the cubes you use), for length, as in Challenge B, volume, as in Challenge E or surface area, as in Challenge H. They also help to develop spatial visualization – interpreting two-dimensional descriptions, as in Challenges D or F or imagining parts that are not seen, as in Challenges A or G. Finally, they provide a context for systematic analysis and reasoning, as in Challenges C, G and H.

A Students will probably think in terms of layers - the top layer has 1 cube, the second 3, the third 6, so the total is 10. An extension is to ask students to build the pattern one layer taller. They may notice that the number of cubes in the layers follows the pattern of "triangular" numbers (1, 3, 6, 10, ...), so called because these numbers of chips or cubes can be arranged in triangular shapes:

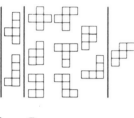

B Interlocking cubes such as Snap Cubes are especially useful for this challenge. You might suggest that students work in pairs to verify their estimates — one child lies on the floor and the other assembles the train. For accuracy, have students put their feet vertically against a wall. Counting is much easier and more accurate if students then break the long train into tens and ones.

C Students will need to organize their search in order to find all patterns. They might first look for all the patterns which have all five in a row, then those with almost four in a row, then three, and finally, two. (There are 12 in all.) These patterns are sometimes called *pentominoes*. The challenge can be changed to find patterns with three, four, or six cubes. Students who are familiar with computer games might realize that the game "Tetris" involves *tetrominoes*, or patterns made from four cubes. Another challenging extension is to ask how many "sculptures" can be made from five cubes, where they need not all lie flat on a page.

D This is more of a challenge if students are not able to handle a die or fold up a copy of the pattern. Students might like to examine commercial dice. Are they all like this pattern? Can students predict the number on the bottom of the die by looking at the number on top? (Yes, since the sum of numbers on opposite faces is always 7.)

E This can be done by what mathematicians call "brute force," by actually building the staircase, but the problem can be simplified. First, if students find the cubes needed for a staircase just one cube wide, they need only multiply the result by 3. They can count the cubes by adding, $1 + 2 + 3 + ... + 9 + 10$. This can be computed directly, or regrouped as $(1 + 10) + (2 + 9) + (3 + 8) + (4 + 7) + (5 + 6) = 5 \times 11 = 55$. If students draw $N + 1$ the one-cube-wide staircase on graph paper, they can give a visual meaning to this trick — moving the striped part of the staircase into the striped area shows that the cubes fill a 5-by-11 rectangle. They might then see that if one wants to find the sum of the numbers up to N, $1 + 2 + 3 + ... + N$, the corresponding rectangle is always $N + 1$ (horizontally) by N (vertically), and so the Nth triangular number is half of the area of this rectangle, or

$$1/2 \times N \times (N + 1).$$

F Here is an oblique view of such a building.

together with a way of recording it on a "floor plan" by the number of cubes which need to be placed above each square. Students can make up their own versions of puzzles, by first making a building, then recording it on a floor plan, and finally drawing it. They may find it easier to draw if they use "isometric grid paper, as shown.

floor plan

2	3	1	1
0	0	0	1

G The 8-corner cubes will be painted on three faces. A cube in the middle of each of the 12 edges will be painted on two faces. A cube in the middle of each of the 6 faces will be painted on one face. There is one cube in the center which will not be painted at all.

To check that all cubes have been counted, add $8 + 12 + 6 + 1 = 27 = 3^3$, the number of small cubes in the original cube. A challenging extension of this problem is to ask the same question when the original cube is cut into 4 x 4 x 4 cubes, or 5 x 5 x 5, etc. There are many nice patterns to be found in this investigation.

H All sculptures made with 6 centimeter cubes will have volume 6 cm³. Students might try to find the surface area by counting the number of exposed faces visible from each side, top, and bottom, or by examining each cube's contribution to the surface area. Possibly an easier way to think of it is to realize that to start with, before the cubes are joined, each cube has surface area 6 cm², making a total of 36 cm² for the six cubes. Each time two cubes are fastened together along a surface, 2 cm² are "lost." To get a surface area of 22 cm², you must "lose" 14 cm² to "gluing," and so 7 faces must adjoin. There are many ways to do this. One is drawn here. Part b is impossible. By the argument above, the surface area of these sculptures is always an even number.

CHALLENGE SET : 7

attribute sets

An attribute set is a collection of materials which vary in a limited number of ways, called the "attributes" of the set. One commonly used attribute set consists of colored shapes, where the attributes are size (large and small), shape (circle, square, diamond and triangle) and color (red, blue, green and yellow). Every possible combination of size, color and shape is represented, and there are no duplicates.

A. Guess the Rule

Some pieces go inside the loop.

Some pieces go outside the loop.

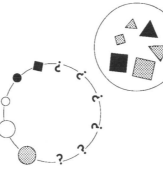

B. What's Missing?

C. Label the Loops

Find labels so that all of the pieces are correctly placed.

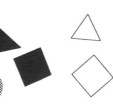

D. Differences

Each piece on this string differs from its neighbor by exactly one attribute.

Place pieces from the loop over the "?'s" to complete the string.

E. How Many Pieces?

Here are some pieces from an attribute set. Assuming that all values of each attribute are shown, how many pieces are in this set?

F. A Difference Puzzle

Put pieces on the dots to solve this puzzle.

Pieces which are connected by one line differ by one attribute, pieces which are conected by two lines differ by two attributes, and so on.

G. What Could Come Next?

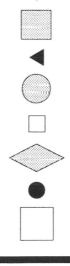

H. What's Missing?

This collection of solids is an attribute set with one piece missing. What is the missing solid?

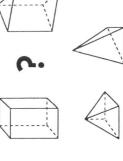

The Mathematical Toolbox   © 1992 Cuisenaire Company of America, Inc.

Commentary:7
ATTRIBUTE SETS

Attribute sets are used to develop thinking processes — classification, recognizing and forming patterns, forming and verifying hypotheses — which are helpful in many aspects of mathematics. Many attribute set problems can be adapted to exercise those same processes in the context of varied mathematics topics. (For example, Challenges A and C could relate to numbers or shapes.)

Most challenges below are stated for the standard attribute set of colored shapes. For these you might want to cut out colored cardboard pieces, put magnetized tape on their backs, and use them to display the problems on a metal-backed chalkboard or cookie sheet. All of the challenges can be adapted for other attribute sets, commercial or teacher/student-made. Encourage children to make up adaptations of these challenges.

You can design attribute sets to involve specific mathematics topics (such as the solids in Challenge H). Students can also design their own attribute sets. For example, they might come up with the idea of the set in Challenge E. The photocopy machine makes it easy to make precise copies. They could first draw the face outline with hair and eyebrows: make three copies of this, then draw in different mouths. Make three copies of these, then add eyes. Finally, make two copies and color in the hair in half of them. If another attribute of size is desired, the whole set can be enlarged or reduced.

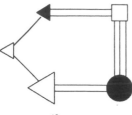

For further ideas on uses of Attribute Pieces, see Chapter 1 of Teaching Mathematics in the Elementary School by David J. Fuys and Rosamond Welchman-Tischler.

A Encourage children to show that they have a solution to this one by having them place another piece either inside or outside the loop. This has the advantage of giving further hints to other students without giving the solution away completely. Added drama is provided by writing the rule ("small," in this case) on a label which is turned over. Students can check themselves by looking at the label. More challenging are labels such as "not square."

B Be sure to discuss how children find their answers. Some might count the number of pieces of each shape, to find that while there are 6 circles, 6 diamonds and 6 squares, and only 5 triangles, which suggests that a triangle is missing. A closer look indicates that there is no large striped triangle. Others might start with color, or size. If you have movable pieces, you might challenge students at first to find the missing piece without moving the pieces, then after a few days, allow physical manipulation of the shapes. When they are arranged in a grid (maybe shapes in rows across, colors in columns up and down), the missing piece is easier to see. (For a similar but simpler challenge, see A Deck of Cards, Set 10, Challenge A.)

C The labels could be "large" and "not circular." Students could also describe the right hand loop in other ways, perhaps "straight sides" or "polygon." This challenge is easy for children to design, and can be extended to three loops.

D A solution is shown to the right. If this challenge is too difficult, replace one or more "?'s" with a piece. A nice further challenge is to use up the entire set of attribute pieces in a large string. These strings are sometimes called "one-difference trains."

E There are 3 mouth positions. For each mouth position there are 3 eye positions, and so there are 9 possible combinations of eye and mouth positions. Finally, hair can be black or white, so there are 2 × 9 = 18 faces.

F This challenge may be easier if you display five pieces that can be used. An easy way to construct such a puzzle is to select five pieces, put them where the dots are, and then draw connecting lines to show the number of ways in which pairs of pieces are different. To the right is shown how this problem was made. To give a hint, simply put one piece in place. Students can easily make up more challenges like this.

G To solve this challenge, students must find some pattern. They may notice the large-small alternation, but color and shape follow no obvious pattern. If asked how successive pieces differ, they will observe that each piece has different size, color and shape from its neighbors. In the terminology of problem D, this is a "three-difference train."

H This is a lovely set of solids to construct and let students manipulate. There are three attributes: shape of base (square or triangle), height (short or tall), and form (prism or pyramid). If students physically sort the pieces by shape of base, they will find that a short, square-based prism is missing. Such experiences encourage students to notice and describe properties of solids, perhaps before they know the formal terminology for the solids.

Students could be challenged to build the set themselves. To make this easier, provide the pieces cut out of cardstock which can be taped together: for the bases, six each of a square and equilateral triangle, all sides measuring the same (perhaps 4 cm); for the sides of the prisms, 7 squares, 4 cm on a side, and 7 rectangles, 4 cm by 8 cm; for the sides of the pyramids, 7 equilateral triangles, 4 cm on a side, and 7 isosceles triangles with base 4 cm and other sides 8 cm. (Or challenge students to figure out what shapes are necessary.) The set can be expanded by adding other shapes as bases.

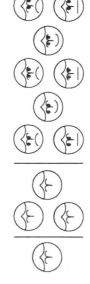

CHALLENGE SET : 8

coins

These challenges use ordinary coins. When you deal with money, you use arithmetic in figuring out the value of your coins, in comparing amounts, in checking change, etc. These examples show that coins can also be used in a variety of other mathematics topics and in more challenging questions.

A. Coins on a Grid

Take 4 pennies, 4 nickels, 4 dimes and 4 quarters. Arrange them on the squares so that there is one of each coin in each row and in each column.

(Now each row and column has the *same* value. Can you arrange the coins so that each row and column has a *different* value?)

B. Two Riddles

I have two coins that total 30¢. One is not a quarter. What are they?

I have twice as many nickels as dimes, and three more cents than nickels. I have 47¢. What coins do I have?

C. A Choice

Which would you rather have, a stack of pennies as tall as you are, or a row of pennies that is as long as the hallway?

D. Differences

In how many ways could you have 33¢ in change?

E. Making Change

I have only dimes and quarters.

I have $2.00.

I have 11 coins.

How many dimes do I have?

F. A Row of Pennies

In how many ways can you arrange five pennies in a row, where each penny can show heads or tails?

Repeat for 3 pennies, 4 pennies, 6 pennies, ... Is there a pattern?

G. Averages

The average date of my collection of 10 pennies was 1982.

Then I found two more pennies, and now the average date of my penny collection is 1983.

What could be the dates of the coins I found?

H. A Jar of Coins

One-fifth of the coins in my jar are dimes.

One-sixth are nickels.

One-tenth are quarters, and the rest are pennies.

The total value is $3.52.

How many of each coin do I have?

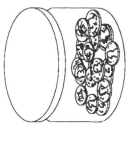

Coins can be viewed in many ways. Pennies are an inexpensive and appealing manipulative, and the fact that they are discs, uniform in size, is used to develop measurement of length in Challenge C. Coins also have different values, and so can be used to pose a wide range of numerical problems as in Challenges A, B, C, E and H. Their two sides are different, which makes them useful for tossing and investigating probability. They can also be used for organized counting, as in Challenge F. (They can also be used as in Two Color Counters, Set 5, or for developing weight, as in Measurement, Set 24, Challenge D.) Finally, they each show the year that they were minted, and these dates can be used in statistical investigations, as in Challenge G.

You might be concerned about having real coins available in your classroom. Some teachers use the handling of money as a way to teach children to be responsible, and to practice counting when they sign out and sign in a certain collection of coins. For all except the last challenge, you can of course use play money, but for small denominations, this may be more expensive than the real thing.

Coins provide a natural link between computation and arithmetic. The structure of 1's, 5's, 10's and 25's in our everyday coinage can be helpful in mental computations. The challenges involve a variety of types of reasoning and illustrate how computational practice can be provided while children are tackling non-routine problems, using higher order thinking skills. As usual, most of these challenges can be used as models for children to create more challenges of their own. Many other challenge sets in the book also use the context of money to pose problems.

A Solutions are shown. The first part of this challenge can be done with any 4 sets of 4 identical objects, such as colored chips or buttons.

B In the first riddle, the statement "One is not a quarter" is not the same as "Neither are quarters." The coins are a quarter and a nickel. This question encourages children to think carefully about language. Students can do the second riddle by trial and error, or approach it through reasoning. The number of cents must be 2, 7, 12, ... Since there are 3 more cents than nickels, there cannot be 2 cents. If there are 7 cents there must be 4 nickels, which would make 27¢. There are half as many dimes as nickels. If there are 2 dimes, the total would be 47¢. The problem is solved.

C This problem lends itself to various strategies. Students who know their height in centimeters might find out about how many pennies you need to make a stack 1 centimeter tall. Likewise they might be able to count floor tiles in the hallway, and find out how many pennies laid end to end are as long as a floor tile. Investigating this problem in this way will give practice with multiplication.

D There are 18 ways. To find them all, it helps to make an organized list, possibly in a chart. It also helps to see that this is the same number of ways as for making 30¢ in change, since to have 33¢ one must always have at least 3 cents.

Amount	25	10	5	1
33¢	1	0	1	3
33¢	1	0	0	8
33¢	0	3	0	3
33¢	0	2	2	3

E This can be done by trial and error, but some reasoning will help. Students might think as follows. There have to be an even number of quarters. (Why?) At the extremes, one could have $2.00 by having all quarters and no dimes (8 coins) or all dimes and no quarters (20 coins). Starting from the all quarter situation, each time you replace 2 quarters by five dimes, you gain three coins. This leads to the solution, 6 quarters and 5 dimes. This is a version of the "cows and chickens" problem described in the Introduction.

F There are 32 ways. They can be found by making an organized list, or possibly by noticing a pattern: There are 2 ways for 1 penny, 4 ways for 2 (HH,HT,TH, TT), 8 ways for 3 pennies. This suggests that the number of ways doubles each time another penny is added. Students can also figure out that there are 32 ways by applying the counting principle, seeing that there are 2 possibilities for the 1st coin, 2 for the 2nd, 2 for the 3rd, 2 for the 4th, and 2 for the 5th and so $2 \times 2 \times 2 \times 2 \times 2 = 16$ in all. It is interesting to elicit all of these different strategies to convince students that different approaches to some problems are both possible and interesting. They can also discuss which is the most pleasing, or which is the easiest to understand.

G It helps to work backwards, using the meaning of "mean." Students might reason that the sum of the dates on the original 10 pennies was $10 \times 1982 = 19,820$. The sum of the dates on the new collection is $12 \times 1983 = 23,796$. Thus the sum of the dates of the two new coins is $23,796 - 19,820 = 3,976$. If you give this problem in 1991, the only possibilities are that both are 1988, or one is 1987 and the other is 1989, or one is 1986 and the other is 1990, or that one is 1985 and the other is 1991. The possibilities will increase as new coins are minted in future years.

If students become interested in looking at dates on coins, they might like to try to graph dates of coins from a large collection of pennies. A moving story based on this idea is *The Hundred Penny Box* by Sharon Bell Mathis, which suggests keeping a collection of pennies, one minted in each year of one's life.

H This can be done algebraically — let x be the number of coins in the jar, then x/5 are dimes, x/6 are quarters, and (x−x/5 − x/6 are nickels, x/10 are quarters, and (x−x/5 − x/6 −x/10) are pennies. You can set up the equation: 352 = 10(x/5) + 5(x/6) + 25(x/10) + 1(x − x/5 − x/6 − x/10), and solve it to find that x = 60, and there are 12 dimes, 10 nickels, 6 quarters, 32 pennies. You can also reason that the number of coins in the jar is divisible by 5, 6 and 10. Check the possibilities, 30, 60, 90, ...

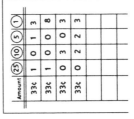

25	10	1	5		25	25	25	25
10	25	5	1		10	10	10	5
1	5	25	10		5	10	5	1
5	1	10	25		5	1	1	1

CHALLENGE SET : 9

toothpicks

This set of problems uses a simple manipulative — toothpicks. Actually any small sticks of uniform length can be used — for example you can cut up coffee stirrers. Toothpicks or coffee stirrers which have flat sides have the advantage of not rolling off a table so easily.

A. What Can You Make?

Take 6 toothpicks. Arrange them on paper. What can you make with them?

Can you make a star with exactly 6 toothpicks?

B. Making Triangles

Take 12 toothpicks.
Use them all to make a triangle.
Then use them all to make two triangles.
Then use them all to make three triangles.

Can you make any other numbers of triangles?

C. Crossings

Toothpicks can be put vertically on these lines. If it is done like this: there are 12 crossing points, as marked.

Put toothpicks on the lines to make the following numbers of crossing points:

4, 15, 16, 21

Find a number you cannot make.

D. Tricky Questions

How can you make 11 toothpicks into 9 (without removing any)?

How can you make 3 toothpicks into 9 (without breaking them!)?

How can you take 1 from 9 and get 10?

E. Removing Toothpicks

Here there are 17 toothpicks.

Remove 6 to leave exactly 2 squares.

F. A Toothpick Puzzle

I used 50 toothpicks to make some squares (like ☐) and triangles (like △).

I made 15 shapes.

How many squares did I make?

G. More Triangles

Use 12 toothpicks to make triangles. Toothpicks cannot overlap, cannot be broken, and must lie entirely on s des of a triangle. Can you make these?

- 1 equilateral triangle
- 2 non-congruent equilateral triangles
- 1 isosceles triangle (not equilateral)
- 2 non-congruent isosceles triangles
- 1 right triangle
- 2 non-congruent right triangles

H. Eight Toothpicks

Take 8 toothpicks, and use them to make squares, with no leftover parts.

What is the least number of squares that you can make? What is the greatest number?

(Hint: the greatest number is more than ten.)

The Mathematical Toolbox   © 1992 Cuisenaire Company of America, Inc.

An amazing variety of puzzles can be posed using small sticks of equal length, such as toothpicks. These puzzles provide a nice context for reasoning and exercising spatial skills. They often appear in books of recreational mathematics which indicates how appealing they can be to children. The challenges in this set might suggest to your students some approaches to creating their own. You can find more toothpick problems in these three sources — each of which has many other wonderful mathematical challenges.

Marilyn Burns, The I Hate Mathematics! Book. As is stated on page 56, "Listen, toothpicks could keep you mathematically busy through a case of bronchial pneumonia!"

Brian Bolt, The Amazing Mathematical Amusement Arcade. Here toothpicks are replaced by match sticks, and puzzles appear throughout the book.

Provoking Thoughts ("The Magazine Devoted to the Thinker in All of Us") published bimonthly by I.D.E.A. Inc., P.O. Box 1004, Austin, MN 55912. This magazine has a regular column, "Toothpick Territory," in addition to many other thought-provoking ideas for children, parents and teachers.

A If you have students glue their six-toothpick constructions onto small pieces of cardboard, you can use them for sorting or "guess my rule" activities. (See Guess My Rule, Set 17, Challenges A–H.) Some possible rules might be: have overlapping toothpicks; contain a triangle; have two or more parallel toothpicks. You could also select four such cards, and ask "Which one is different? Why?" If students examine different ways in which others use toothpicks, they might be more likely to come up with a star made from 6 unbroken toothpicks.

B Students might think about this problem in terms of arithmetic. Since a triangle has 3 sides, to make an equilateral triangle with 12 toothpicks, you need 12 ÷ 3 = 4 toothpicks on a side. But the triangle need not be equilateral — the sides might be made from 3, 4 and 5 toothpicks (which yields a right triangle), or from 5, 5 and 2 toothpicks (which yields an isosceles triangle). Those are the only ways to make one triangle with 12 toothpicks, although students may need to try out other combinations to realize this. There are several ways to make 2 or 3 triangles, as shown. If toothpicks are allowed to overlap, many triangles can be made. For example, one might make 2 of the 6-pointed stars shown in Challenge A to get 16 triangles.

C You might need to explain that toothpicks have to cross all the segments in their path, so a given toothpick crosses either 2 or 5 segments. This problem can be thought of arithmetically — how can you make the numbers of crossing points as sums of multiples of 2 and 5? 4 = 2 × 2; 15 = 3 × 5; 16 = 8 × 2; 21 = 3 × 5 + 3 × 2. Some can be made in more than one way (for example, 15 can be made with 3 toothpicks vertically on 5 segments, or with 1 toothpick on 5 and 3 toothpicks on 2 segments. It is impossible to place toothpicks on these lines to make 1 or 3 crossings. You can however make any even number, and any other odd number (because if you subtract 5 from an odd number greater than or equal to 5, the result will be even). Note how this challenge and Challenge F are variations on the "cows and chickens" problem discussed in the Introduction of this book.

D These all involve numerals.

NINE IX |X ← remove this one.

E You can think about this problem by reasoning that the solution will have two squares made with 11 toothpicks. One of the squares will have to use 8 toothpicks, and the other is formed with 3 extras, which means that the 2 squares will share one side. As a challenge, can you remove other numbers of toothpicks to leave exactly 2 squares?

F This is a variation of the classic "cows and chickens" problem described in the Introduction of this book. It can be solved by many strategies, including trial and error. One way to find a solution by reasoning is to think that if all of the 15 shapes made were triangles, there would be 45 toothpicks. This is 5 less than the number of toothpicks used, so the 5 extra toothpicks could be used to make 5 of the triangles into squares, resulting in a solution of 5 squares and 10 triangles. (Can you use the same reasoning on the "cows and chickens" problem?)

G This challenge extends Challenge B and involves classification of triangles by lengths of sides. You can extend the list of challenges if you wish. The 12 toothpicks can make 1 equilateral triangle, (4,4,4), or 2 non-congruent ones, (1,1,1) and (3,3,3). One isosceles triangle is (5,5,2), and 2 isosceles triangles are (3,3,1) and (2,2,1). One right triangle is (3,4,5), but no others can be made with only 12 units. Students who know the Pythagorean Theorem for right triangles can check that there are no smaller whole number solutions to the equation $a^2 + b^2 = c^2$. If you want to include more impossible things to build with 12 toothpicks, include one of these:

two non-congruent scalene triangles
two congruent isosceles triangles (not equilateral)

Challenge your students to explain why these are impossible, and to come up with more.

H Finding the least possible number of squares you can make with 8 toothpicks is easy — it is one, with 2 toothpicks on a side. Two squares is also easy. To make 3 squares, students must be encouraged to overlap toothpicks. To make many more, try overlapping as much as possible. The arrangement to the right contains 14 squares, of three different sizes.

CHALLENGE SET : 10

a deck of cards

These challenges concern a standard deck of playing cards. There are an amazing number of games, tricks and puzzles that can be done with this set of 52 pieces of cardboard, and they have a long and rich history and literature.

Do you play any card games that make you think?

A. What's Missing?

7♠ 7◇ 5♥
5♠ 6◇ 7♣
6♥ 5◇ 6♠
5♣ 6♣

B. Twelve Hearts

I picked 3 cards from a new deck of cards.

There were 12 hearts in all.

What could the cards have been?

C. Upside Down

How many cards look *just* the same upside down as they do right side up? (Another way to say this is, how many cards have *rotational symmetry?*)

How many cards have *line symmetry?*

D. How Many Hearts?

In a complete deck of cards, how many hearts actually appear?

(*Note: there are more than 3 hearts on the three of hearts.*)

Is the answer the same for all decks?

E. A Tricky Deal

You have all of the hearts in a deck of cards. You deal them as follows — first put a card down, then put the next to the back of the deck, then put the next down, then put the next to the back of the deck, and so on.

How should the cards be arranged at the start so that they end up in order?

A 2 3 4 5 6 7 8 9 10 J Q K

F. Scoring

In some games, cards are scored like this:

- Ace is worth 1,
- Cards from 2 to 10 are scored by their face value, and
- Jack, Queen and King are all worth ten points.

How much is the entire deck of cards worth?

G. Pick a Card

Pick a card from 1 to 10.
Double it.
Add 6.
Add the original card's number.
Divide by 3.
Subtract the original card's number.
What do you get?

Try another. Explain.

H. Twenty-one

Arrange these cards in this array.

Pick any four cards so that no two are in the same row and no two are in the same column.

Add the values of the cards.

Do this again. Do this once more.

What do you notice?

6♥	3♥	5♥	4♥
9♥	6◇	8♥	7♥
5◇	2♥	4♣	3
7◇	4◇	6♣	5♣

The Mathematical Toolbox   © 1992 Cuisenaire Company of America, Inc.

Commentary:10
A DECK OF CARDS

Playing cards are an easily available and familiar experience of number. Children use mathematics in many card games, when adding up scores, as in Challenge F or H, or when using logical thinking and/or probability to plan moves. The deck of cards itself has the structure of an attribute set (see Attribute Sets, Set 7) which is used in Challenge A. Individual cards have visual structures (used in Challenges C and D). Manipulation of cards can encourage students to "play around" with mathematical relationships in an enjoyable context.

For very young children, regular playing cards might be misleading, because, for example, the "4 of hearts" has 6 hearts. Simplified cards, with just the numeral and the corresponding pictured set, are easily made with small stickers or rubber stamps. The uses of many card games for learning mathematics are described in Group Games in Early Education, Implications of Piaget's Theory, by Kamii and Devries (NAEYC, 1980). A use of old playing cards for young children is to make a puzzle which practices matching of set to numeral. Just cut out the symbols of the suits in the middle of the card with a razor blade.

A To present this problem, you might fasten the indicated cards to the board with masking tape or magnetic tape. At first, present them mixed up, in no particular order. As a hint, after a day or so, let a child arrange them in some way. If the cards are organized in a systematic way, as shown to the right, children are more likely to see the structure of the set of cards. If children enjoy this problem, increase the challenge by using more suits and more numbers.

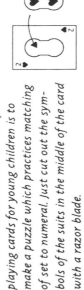

B At first it may seem that there are several possible solutions to this problem since 12 = 1 + 2 + 9 = 1 + 3 + 8 = 2 + 3 + 7, etc. But on most decks of cards, there are two extra images of the suit in the corners of the cards, so the "2 of hearts" in fact has 4 hearts. The cards *must be* Ace, 2 and 3 of hearts.

C There are 36 cards which look exactly the same upside down (assuming all are printed perfectly, in the center of the cards) — all even cards from 2 to 10, all Kings, Queens and Jacks and the Ace, 3, 5, and 9 of diamonds. (Do you see why the others don't work? Of the four symbols for suits, only the diamond itself has rotational symmetry, and so the symbol in the middle of an odd array prevents the entire pattern from having rotational symmetry.) This may vary from deck to deck — you'd better check your deck. No cards have line symmetry.

D On many decks, Ace has 3 hearts, 2 has 4, 3 has 5, etc. King, Queen and Jack each have 4 hearts, so there are (3 + 4 + 5 + ... + 12) + 12 = 75 + 12 = 87. (On other decks there are lots more little hearts in the clothing on the face cards.) You might ask students to check if this answer is correct for decks at home.

E There are various ways to tackle this problem. One is to start with the cards in order from Ace to King, and see how they come out if you deal them in the way described. This is the result.

A 3 5 7 9 J K 4 8 Q 6 2 10

This tells you that in the initial ordering, if the cards will be dealt in order, 2 must be in the 3rd place, 3 must be in the 7th place, and so forth.

Another strategy is to make spaces for the cards in the desired arrangement, and start filling in every other space with the cards in the desired final order:

A _ 2 _ 3 _ 4 _ 5 _ 6 _ 7

When you get to the last space, go back to the beginning, but remember to leave a blank space between each space filled in (so 8 will go between 2 and 3). The final order is A, Q, 2, 8, 3, J, 4, 9, 5, K, 6, 10, 7.

You can extend this challenge by proposing other types of deal — maybe putting two at the back of the deck each time. Which strategy is easiest for finding the new shuffle?

This problem — and many other wonderful ones — are presented in an appealing way for children in Part 4, Logical Puzzles, of *Math for Smarty Pants* by Marilyn Burns.

F Find the sum for each suit. For the cards Ace through 10, the sum is:

1 + 2 + 3 + 4 + 5 + 6 + 7 + 8 + 9 + 10 = 55.

Add 30 for face cards, to get 85. For all 4 suits, the sum is 4 × 85 = 340.

G You always get 2. To explain why, a student might represent the chosen card as a rectangle. Then the steps in the procedure become:

This last amount is to be shared among 3:

Each share is the original card and two more, so when the card's number is subtracted, the result is always 2. This pictorial symbolism leads naturally to a more formal algebraic explanation for why $(2N + 6 + N) \div 3 - N = 2$.

H You always get 21. This works because the array is an addition table with 4, 1, 3, 2 across the top and 2, 5, 1, 3 down the side. The suits don't matter. You can make up other card arrays which will work for this trick by forming addition tables with other numbers.

+	4	1	3	2
2	6	3	5	4
5	9	6	8	7
1	5	2	4	3
3	7	4	6	5

CHALLENGE SET : 11

a bag of nuts

These challenges require a bag of mixed unshelled nuts, such as those pictured below. For Challenges D and E you will need to shell some nuts.

F. Average Price of Nuts

What is the average price per nut if a pound of mixed nuts costs $1.49?

What is the average price per walnut if a pound of walnuts also costs $1.49?

WALNUTS $1.49

MIXED NUTS $1.49

G. Mystery Bag of Nuts

My bag contains 32 nuts — only pecans, walnuts and peanuts.

There are twice as many walnuts as pecans.

There are two more peanuts than walnuts.

Exactly what is in the bag?

H. Mixing Nuts

Pecans cost $4 per pound, almonds cost $3 per pound, walnuts cost $2 per pound and peanuts cost $1 per pound.

You want to make a mixture containing all of these types of nuts, which costs $2 per pound. How could you do this?

C. Nuts in a Cup

Use unshelled nuts.

How many cups could you fill up with all of these nuts?

How many walnuts would fit in the cup?

How many almonds would fit in the cup?

D. Nutmeats and Shells

What fraction of the weight of the whole peanut is shell? Is this the same for the other types of nuts?

How many grams of whole peanuts do you need to get 100 grams of shelled peanuts?

E. Shopping for Nuts—Shelled or Unshelled?

The one pound bag of mixed unshelled nuts costs $1.49.

A 12-ounce can of shelled mixed nuts costs $2.69.

Which is the better buy?

What do you need to know to answer this question?

A. Favorite Nuts

What kind of nut is there the most of?

Which nut do you think most students in the class will like best?

Can every student have the nut he or she likes best?

B. Comparing Nuts

Use unshelled nuts.

Which is the heaviest nut? How could you find out?

Which is the biggest nut? How could you find out?

Is the heaviest also the biggest?

A BAG OF NUTS

These challenges show how mathematics concepts can be found in a collection of everyday objects. Nuts are durable, relatively inexpensive, and easy to find. Nuts are especially interesting from the point of view of price comparison, since a little research in a grocery store will give the prices per pound of various types of nuts (peanuts, walnuts, almonds, pecans, etc.), as well as the prices shelled or unshelled. Nuts are pleasant to handle, and have interesting variations in shape, volume and weight, not to mention taste. They are also healthy to eat (except for those with allergies). After their mathematical investigations with the nuts, students can use the nuts to bake a cake. The empty walnut shells can be used to make the bodies for little turtles — glue on cardboard bases as shown. These turtles are useful for students who work with the computer language LOGO. Students can move the nut-turtles around on a table top and act out the commands they create in LOGO which tell a "turtle" on the screen how to move.

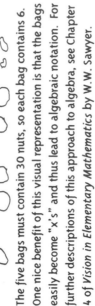

Many other collections of objects, edible or non-edible, can be used in some of the same ways that the nuts are in these challenges. A few suggestions are: collections of natural objects such as shells, or acorns and other wild seeds; bags of mixed candy; a bag of mixed balloons; "trail mix" of dried fruit and nuts; mixed nails and screws from the hardware store.

A This challenge might be accompanied by slips of paper on which children can write their names and answers. If children have seen graphs before, this question might motivate them to make a graph. Otherwise use this challenge as an opportunity to

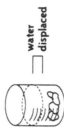

develop bar graphs. If you use a large bag of nuts for this, the numbers might get quite large. You might have children make their individual estimates, and then when it is time to check, split the class up into groups and give each group a share of the bag to sort onto a grid and then graph. If your students are working on tens and ones, provide small cups in which ten nuts can be placed. Children will enjoy the taste test. They may also be surprised that in a blindfold test they like different types of nuts than they expected.

B Available scales may not be sufficiently sensitive to compare single nuts. Children can be led to count out the same number of each nut and use a balance scale to compare the groups. To measure volume, children can measure water in a cup, add some nuts, and see how much water was displaced.

water displaced

C This challenge should be presented with a small plastic cup placed next to the unopened bag. Students might be given a day for each estimate, before the result is checked. They should see relations among the estimates. For example about three times more almonds will fit in the cup than walnuts, if a walnut is about three times as large as an almond. (Students might try to combine a cup of walnuts with a cup of almonds and discover that "1 + 1" is not always 2.)

D This challenge provides practice in measurement, possibly in grams. Students might initially look at just one shelled peanut, with its shell, and make an estimate. To get an accurate answer, have students shell a large number of peanuts and weigh both nuts and their shells. Once students have found out how much of the unshelled nut is actually nutmeat, they might be interested to compare prices of shelled and unshelled nuts of the same type.

E Students should realize that many questions need to be asked in the approach to this challenge. Is the nut mix in the bag of unshelled nuts the same as that

in the jar of shelled nuts? How much of the weight of an unshelled nut is the shell? (See Challenge D.) How much should one pay for the labor of shelling the nuts? How long does it take to shell a bag with a nutcracker? Do unshelled nuts taste the same as those in the jar? They might be less seasoned or roasted. All of these questions suggest techniques of sampling, counting, estimation. To add a sense of reality, use current prices from local stores.

F To answer these questions, students must estimate how many nuts are in both bags. Compare this challenge with Challenge H.

G Before presenting this challenge, prepare a "mystery bag" containing the correct mixture of nuts. The answer can then be secretly checked by students who think they have a solution. Students might approach this by trial and error — "Maybe there are 5 pecans, which would mean there are 10 walnuts, and 12 peanuts. That would make a total of 27 nuts — too small, I'd better try more pecans." A visual approach might be to draw a little bag showing the pecans. Walnuts are represented by two bags with the same number as in the pecan bag, and peanuts by two more bags and 2 loose nuts. And so the total of 32 nuts is shown as

The five bags must contain 30 nuts, so each bag contains 6. One nice benefit of this visual representation is that the bags easily become "x's" and thus lead to algebraic notation. For further descriptions of this approach to algebra, see Chapter 4 of *Vision in Elementary Mathematics* by W.W. Sawyer.

H Students may have varied strategies and solutions. Since walnuts cost $2 per lb., it doesn't matter how many walnuts are in the mix. Students might reason that 1 lb. at $4 and 2 lbs. at $6, the right price. Also 1 lb. at $3 and 1 lb. at $1 gives 2 lbs. at $4, the right price. So a solution would be to mix 1 lb. pecans, 1 lb. almonds, any amount of walnuts and 3 lbs. peanuts. Students might be interested in thinking about how much profit they could make if the quantities were altered.

Name ___

which has greatest number?

which is liked most?

can every child have favorite? ___

CHALLENGE SET : 12

calculators

For these challenges, use an ordinary four-function calculator.

The "four functions" are addition, subtraction, multiplication and division. But there are probably other keys as well. Explore the calculator. Can you figure out what every key does?

A. Six

Use only these keys

| 4 | 7 | + | – | = |

to get a display of 6.

B. Equals Equals Equals

First, try pushing this key sequence:

| 2 | + | 3 | = | = | = |

What's happening?
If your calculator keeps changing as you continue, try this:

- I punched 4 keys. The calculator shows 9.
- You punch = again, it shows 13.
- You punch = again, it shows 17.
- What 4 keys did I punch at the start?

C. A Sticky Computation

Which store has the better buy?

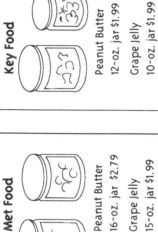

Met Food

Peanut Butter
16-oz. jar $2.79

Grape Jelly
15-oz. jar $1.99

Key Food

Peanut Butter
12-oz. jar $1.99

Grape Jelly
10-oz. jar $1.99

D. Comparing Calculators

Compare two calculators.
Find as many ways as you can in which they are different.

Are the keys the same?
Do they work in the same ways?

E. Make the Calculator Lie!

Enter the smallest number that you can on the calculator. Divide it by 2.
What should you get? What do you get?

Do this calculation: $(1 \div 3) \times 3 = ?$
What should you get? What do you get?
Find another way to make the calculator lie.

F. Seven Sevens

How can you get .7777777 on the calculator display by pressing the | 7 | key no more than once?

Can you do it using only 4 key presses?

G. Memories . . .

Try this key sequence. Write down the numbers you get.

| 1 | M+ | + | MR | M+ | + | MR | M+ |
| + | MR | M+ | + | M+ | + | MR | M+ |

(keep repeating this)

What is the pattern? Why do these numbers appear?

H. Roots

a. The calculator can find $\sqrt{2}$ (the *square root* of 2), which is a number whose square is 2. Enter 2 and push the $\sqrt{\ }$ key many times. What happens?
Enter any number, push the $\sqrt{\ }$ key 30 times. What happens?

b. Use the calculator to find $\sqrt[3]{2}$ (the *cube root* of 2), which is a number whose cube is 3.

Commentary: 12
CALCULATORS

Calculators open up exciting mathematical possibilities for children. Writers who work on a word processor may find it difficult to imagine spending time laboriously writing by hand, correcting, and using a printed dictionary to check spelling. Of course they could, but it would take time away from their flow of ideas. Calculators (and at a higher level, computers) are similarly tools which allow wider scope for higher order thinking in mathematics. The National Council of Mathematics, in its Curriculum and Evaluation Standards for School Mathematics, recommends that calculators be available to children throughout their school experience, and that they be used not just to do or check computation, but to engage children in significant mathematical explorations.

This set of challenges provides examples of some appropriate ways in which calculators can be used throughout the mathematics curriculum. They can be used to extend understanding of square and cube roots, as in Challenge G, or of the difference between the calculator's number system and the real numbers as in Challenge E. They provide a context for problem solving, involving thinking skills such as pattern finding, making and testing hypotheses in Challenges B, F and H. They can make students aware of the nature of algorithms as in Challenge B, an important understanding for work with computers. They can help students develop awareness of what technology can and cannot offer. For example, it can help with sticky computations, as in Challenge C, but may be less useful than a little thinking or mental arithmetic, as in Challenge A. The challenges require a four-function calculator. For Challenge B, check that there is the "repeating constant" feature described in the challenge. Inexpensive calculators seem to vary not only in how the various keys are placed and labeled, but also in how certain keys function. This variety can encourage students to analyze and investigate, as in Challenge D.

A One approach is to realize that you can add 1 by following the sequence $\boxed{+}$ $\boxed{7}$ $\boxed{-}$ $\boxed{4}$ $\boxed{=}$. Since 6 is one less than 7, you can get 6 by first entering 7 then doing this sequence. Students might also realize that 6 is 3 + 3 and 3 is 7 − 4, and so the sequence $\boxed{7}$ $\boxed{-}$ $\boxed{4}$ $\boxed{+}$ $\boxed{7}$ $\boxed{-}$ $\boxed{4}$ $\boxed{=}$ will yield 6. The challenge can be varied by changing the target number or keys that can be used.

B Solutions will depend on the calculator. Most four-function calculators have the "repeating constant" feature — the result of pushing the "=" keys in the sequence shown is either 5, 8, 11, or 5, 7, 9. It depends on whether the first or second addend is remembered and repeated. In the first case, the second addend gets added each time the = key is pushed; in the second case, it is the first addend. Assuming it is the first case, then the initial four keys that were punched were $\boxed{5}$ $\boxed{=}$ $\boxed{4}$ $\boxed{=}$.

C This challenge demonstrates that once children understand the concepts underlying multiplication and division, the calculator frees them to answer much more difficult real-world problems than they could otherwise. First they should determine if they want to compare price per ounce of each item or just total cost. Does it make sense to go to different stores for the two items? Perhaps refine the question to ask which store has the better buy per sandwich if a sandwich uses 1 ounce of peanut butter and 1/2 ounce of jelly? Try to use local supermarket advertisements for this one.

D For this you will need to find two calculators which are different, and if possible in ways other than shape, color, size, arrangement of keys, etc. Even within the basic, four-function calculator types there are interesting differences which can provide a context for exploration. Maybe the repeating constant feature works (or doesn't) in different ways. Sometimes the % key does different things. (Do you need to punch "=" after it?)

E The calculator will probably give the results that .0000001 ÷ 2 = 0, not .00000005, and that (1÷3) × 3 = .9999999, not 1. Students should conclude that the calculator's number system is not quite the same as ours,

because it is limited to seven decimal places, and usually just cuts off or 'truncates' any further decimal expansion. Numbers can be too large or too small for the calculator to recognize, or take too many digits. Some more "errors" that calculators make are in dealing with order of operations. The sequence "2 + 3 x 5 =" will yield 25 on most basic calculators, although more elaborate ones will agree with the "correct" answer, 17. In effect, the calculator finds the expression 2 + 3 x 5 the convention about notation gives the expression 2 + 3 x 5 the meaning 2 + (3 x 5). See Challenge H for another "error" involving square roots. Of course these are not really "errors," just differences between calculator arithmetic and our own. Investigation of such differences can deepen students' understanding of our own number system.

F You might want to give a hint. Students probably know that some divisions give patterns: 1÷3 gives 0.3333333. If they explore division by various numbers, they may find a special characteristic of division by 9: 1÷9 = 0.1111111, 2÷9 = 0.2222222, etc. You can extend this challenge by exploring what happens if you divide by 99 or 999 or …. (How could you get the pattern .1717171, pushing 1 and 7 only once each?)

G This gives the Fibonacci sequence, in which each term is the sum of the two terms before it. Students should keep track of what is in the calculator's memory after each step.

H For part a, an initial number greater than 1, will eventually yield 1. An initial number less than 1, yields results very close to 1, but may "get stuck" at 0.9999998. Students can check that, in fact $\sqrt{0.9999998}$ is greater than 0.9999998 — such calculators "round down" the result.

Part b can be done by trial and error. Make a guess for the cube root of 2, say 1.5. Since $1.5^3 = 3.375$, try something smaller, maybe 1.3. The calculator gives $1.3^3 = 2.197$ which is closer but still too large. $1.2^3 = 1.728$, so 1.2 is too small, so try something inbetween. $1.25^3 = 1.953125$ and $1.26^3 = 2.000376$, so try a number between these two, etc. This requires understanding of cube roots and decimal notation.

The Mathematical Toolbox   © 1992 Cuisenaire Company of America, Inc.

CHALLENGE SET : 13

concept cards

In these challenges you are shown some examples and some non-examples of a concept. Based on these, form a hypothesis about the concept, and decide which of the further possibilities are also examples. At the bottom of each concept card add:

Draw something which is a _____.

Draw something which is not a _____.

What is a _____?

A. Fits

These are Fits:

These are not Fits:

Which of these are Fits?

a.   b.   c.   d.   e.

B. Secs

These are Secs:

These are not Secs:

Which of these are Secs?

a.   b.   c.   d.   e.

C. Thids

These are Thids:

R   f   ∈   Q   2

These are not Thids:

6   S   X   C   N

Which of these are Thids?

a.   b.   c.   d.   e.

O   d   n   H   B

D. Furs

These are Furs:

18   207   9   63   315

These are not Furs:

62   8   350   14   31

Which of these are Furs?

a.   b.   c.   d.   e.

27   6   405   45   1305

E. Fifes

These are Fifes:

These are not Fifes:

Which of these are Fifes?

a.   b.   c.   d.   e.

F. Siths

These are Siths:

These are not Siths:

Which of these are Siths?

a.   b.   c.   d.   e.

G. Secs

These are Sens:

$\frac{2}{3}$ $\frac{7}{8}$ $\frac{5}{1}$ $\frac{4}{15}$ $\frac{12}{25}$

These are not Sens:

$\frac{4}{8}$ $\frac{6}{15}$ $\frac{9}{3}$ $\frac{12}{26}$ $\frac{2}{6}$

Which of these are Sens?

a.   b.   c.   d.   e.

$\frac{12}{30}$ $\frac{25}{9}$ $\frac{8}{10}$ $\frac{1}{3}$ $\frac{6}{5}$

H. Egs

These are Egs:

These are not Egs:

Which of these are Egs?

a.   b.   c.   d.   e.

The Mathematical Toolbox

Commentary: 13
CONCEPT CARDS

Students who have experiences with forming and expressing their own definitions before being told them are more likely to understand the role of definition in mathematics. Such experiences will make them more aware of the exact meaning or significance of a word or phrase, and more likely to "take ownership" of the idea and remember it. In addition, a teacher can assess students' natural language if students are asked to use mathematical terms before they are formally reviewed or introduced. This is one reason for using concept cards in the classroom. Also, they are appealing and may motivate students to consider diverse mathematical concepts. Students will exercise higher order thinking skills when noting similarities and differences, and when forming and checking their hypotheses.

The three lines in the left top corner,

Draw something which is a ___.
Draw something which is not a ___.
What is a ___?

were omitted from the challenges only because of space restrictions on the page. When presenting these concept cards individually, write these three lines below them, in order to ensure that students can use and verbalize their definitions.

Concept cards can be used to review a concept previously learned, to introduce a new one, or simply to exercise reasoning powers. Once students understand the format, they can be challenged to make up their own concept cards for their classmates. This task is more difficult than it seems, if one wants to make sure that there is only one possible interpretation. Students should listen to how others interpret their cards, and then refine them so that their idea is communicated.

When you present a concept card as a "weekly challenge," you can give hints by adding an additional example and non-example each day. If students are stuck, you can ask questions directing attention to specific features of the illustrations. Make sure that a child who "sees" a solution quickly doesn't rob other students of the opportunity to think. It helps to encourage students initially to tell you the answer to the question "Which of these are ___'s?" and not the actual definition ("What is a ___?"). When students have formulated a valid hypothesis, encourage them to think about how they came to that idea. Be open to the possibility that there might be more than one "answer," as in Challenge D. You can use such an opportunity to have students refine the selection of examples so that only one of the hypotheses is possible.

For display of these challenges, consider using pictures or cut-outs backed with magnetic tape on a metal-backed board or cookie sheet. The same pictures might be reused to show different concepts. If you and your children enjoy this format, you will find that all sorts of concepts can be formed through a concept card. A few examples: use pictures of vegetables from colorful supermarket handouts to elicit what part of the plant a vegetable is, or if it can be locally grown; use pictures of buildings to elicit observation of architectural details (which houses have something circular in their decoration?) or functions (which buildings are homes?); use names of places to elicit classification as cities or countries, or by their continent.

The "Concept Card" format may be familiar to you as the "Creature Cards" published by the Elementary Science Study in the 1960's. See the teachers' guide that accompanies those materials for further rationale and commentary on their use. Another resource using this idea is Wollygoggles and Other Creatures by Thomas C. O'Brien. See Fractions, Set 25, Challenge A. for another example.

Do you see the pattern in the nonsense names in these cards? (Think of ordinal numbers.)

 A If students are stuck, you can ask what features each creature has, and if anything is the same about features of the fits. Children will then probably notice the triangular noses.

B This is similar to A in that students might be encouraged to look at the faces' features. For secs, however, number of eyes is involved, rather than shape of nose.

C A hint for this one might be to try making letters and numerals with toothpicks (which cannot be curved). This might alert students to looking for straight and curved components of a figure. Thids are composed of both straight and curved parts.

 D This concept card might be viewed as incomplete because there are at least three possible hypotheses which fit the examples shown: Furs could be multiples of three, or multiples of nine, or numbers where the sum of the digits is 9. Students might be challenged to add examples and non-examples to those shown so that two of the hypotheses are ruled out. (Interesting side discussions might lead to realizing that all multiples of 9 are also multiples of 3, but not vice versa, and all numbers whose digits sum to 9 are multiples of 9 but not vice versa.)

 E Teachers have been surprised by which students saw this one. Some students who are weak at computation have considerable spatial intuition and might see that Fifes have a vertical line of symmetry.

 F This is more complicated logically: Siths must be both quadrilateral and striped.

G This shows how concept cards can be used to review a concept previously learned. Discussion of Sens can allow a teacher to assess student vocabulary and understanding about equivalent fractions and fractions in reduced terms.

 H As in G, discussion of Egs shows whether or not the word "parallel" is part of students' active vocabulary, and exactly what they think the term means. A visual hint can be given by taking a pair of chopsticks and placing them on a pair of parallel lines in an Eg, and then on a pair of non-parallel lines in a non-Eg.

CHALLENGE SET : 14

which one is different?

Each challenge shows a collection — of numerals, expressions, letters, figures — and has the same question — "Which one is different?" Each has many possible solutions.

When you have worked through these, try to make up your own which has every item as a possible "different" one.

A. Which One Is Different?

Explain your reasoning.

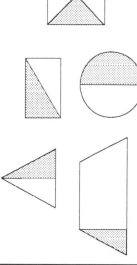

Find more than one possible answer.

B. Which One Is Different?

Explain your reasoning.

4 + 2   4 + 4   2 + 6

10 - 2   7 + 1

4 + 2 + 2

Find more than one possible answer.

C. Which One Is Different?

Explain your reasoning.

A   E   I   Y   O   N

Find more than one possible answer.

D. Which One Is Different?

Explain your reasoning.

Find more than one possible answer.

E. Which One Is Different?

Explain your reasoning.

1   2   4   8   12   6

Find more than one possible answer.

F. Which One Is Different?

Explain your reasoning.

Find more than one possible answer.

G. Which One Is Different?

Explain your reasoning.

25   51   53   55

65   93   135

Find more than one possible answer.

H. Which One Is Different?

Explain your reasoning.

$\sqrt{9}$ 3.9   3.01

$\dfrac{26}{10}$ 3.3333... $\sqrt{10}$

Find more than one possible answer.

The Mathematical Toolbox   © 1992 Cuisenaire Company of America, Inc.

Commentary: 14
WHICH ONE IS DIFFERENT?

When exploring these challenges, students will be led to classify the examples given, to find similarities and differences. In each of the given problems, there is more than one answer. Encourage students to find more than one, in particular, answers other than those indicated below. If students need more encouragement, after a while you might underline the examples which you think they might be able to see as the "different" ones.

Discussion of such problems leads students to value not only "the answer" but also the process of arriving at the answer. When you ask students to explain their thinking about these problems, you will also have an opportunity to determine the extent of their "active" mathematical vocabulary — the terms they use spontaneously — as opposed to their "passive" vocabulary, the terms they respond to when the teacher or text uses them. Their passive vocabulary might be more extensive than their active vocabulary, and teachers may be misled about students' active vocabulary by their performance on tests which do not require them to produce the terms themselves.

Consider using this Which One Is Different? format in connection with any mathematics topic you are introducing or reviewing. The examples given are related to geometry, number and numeration, basic facts, fractions and decimals. Feel free to adapt any of these ideas, or to invent variations. Further uses of this format are shown in Solids, Set 27, Challenge B, and in Halloween, Set 30, Challenge A. It is easy for you and for students to create problems in this format with more than one answer. You can use the same format in other curriculum areas. (For example, which one is different among these: New York; Montreal; London; Kansas? Students might think of number of syllables, continent, city vs. state, ...)

The Children's Television Workshop program "Sesame Street" often uses a format like this with just four images. You may know the song that goes with the puzzles, "One of These Things Is Not Like the Others, ..." For young children, consider using real objects, or pictures related to other curriculum areas. You can also present puzzles of this type on cards, as part of a learning center. Punch holes by each example, and make a mark (such as a "happy face") on the back by the holes corresponding to possible answers. Students are to poke a straw through the hole, and turn the card over to check their response. If they find an answer which they can justify but which is not marked on the back, they should be encouraged to go to the teacher, explain their answer, and then mark it on the back.

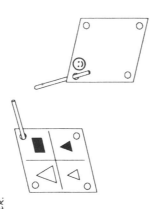

A One is small, while the others are large. One is crosshatched, while the others are not. One has no straight sides, the others do. To present problems like this, you might use large colored shapes. It is convenient to have a set with pieces of magnetic tape on the back, which can be moved around easily on a metal-backed chalkboard or cookie sheet. (Such a set is described in the commentary on Attribute Sets, Set 7.)

B Students should come up with many answers. Only 4 + 2 is not an expression for 8. Only 4 + 4 has all the numbers the same. Only 4 + 2 + 2 has three addends. Only 7 + 1 contains three addends. Only 10 − 2 involves subtraction. Only 2 + 6 has the first digit smaller than the others. This example shows how review of routine skills can be put in a thought-provoking context.

C If students look at the forms as letters, they may say that only N is not always a consonant. If they look at the letters as geometric forms, they may

say that only O contains curves, and that only O doesn't have line symmetry. Would anyone say that only I is not in "anyone?"

D Only one is not a subdivision of a polygon. Only one is divided into four parts. Only one does not have half of its area shaded. This example could be suitable for reviewing the meaning of a fraction.

E Only 12 has two digits. Only 8 is not a factor of 12. Only 1 has only 1 factor. Also, only 1 is a factor of all the other numbers. Only 2 is a prime number. Only 4 has exactly 3 factors. Only 6 comes after a number greater than it.

F Only one of these shapes is not a quadrilateral. Only one does not contain at least one right angle. Only one does not have at least one pair of parallel sides. To give a hint on a problem like this, consider displaying a list of vocabulary words that might be used to describe how one is different. However, it is preferable to wait until students have first had a chance to use their own vocabulary.

G Only 25 is a perfect square. Only 51 is divisible by 17. Only 53 is a prime number. Only 55 repeats a digit. Only 65 contains two consecutive digits. Only 93 does not contain "5" as a digit. Only 135 has three digits. Each of the seven numbers is seen to be the "different one" in some way. As an extension, ask students to come up with their own challenge like this.

H Only $\sqrt{9}$ is a whole number. Only 3.9 would not be rounded to 3 as the nearest whole number. Only 3.01 has two decimal places. Only 26/10 is written as a fraction (although all of the others could be, except for $\sqrt{10}$). Only 3.333... is written as an infinite repeating decimal (although again the others could be, except for $\sqrt{10}$). Only $\sqrt{10}$ is not a rational number (that is, it cannot be written as a fraction, where numerator and denominator are whole numbers). Again, ask students to make up their own challenge using mathematics topics currently being studied.

The Mathematical Toolbox   © 1992 Cuisenaire Company of America, Inc.

CHALLENGE SET : 15

what could come next?

Each of these challenges presents a sequence in which there is a pattern of some sort. Try to find the pattern, and predict what will come next.

Some of the challenges involve numbers and some involve shapes. In the ones that involve both numbers and shapes, try to see how the patterns are related.

A. What Could Come Next?

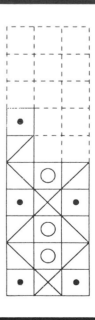

B. What Could Go In the Empty Squares?

C. What Could Come Next?

A B C D E F ? ? !

D. What Could Come Next?

a. 1 6 4 9 7 12 ? ?

b. (number line 0–17)

E. What Could Come Next?

a. 1 3 6 10 15 21 ? ?

b. (block figures) ? ?

c. 1 3 6 9 12 15 ? ?

F. What Could Come Next?

5, 12, 19, 26, 2, 9, 16, 23, ?, ?, ?

G. What Could Come Next?

? ? !

H. What Could Come Next?

a. 0 5 12 21 32 ? ?

b. (grid figures)

The Mathematical Toolbox   © 1992 Cuisenaire Company of America. Inc.

The search for pattern underlies a great deal of mathematical thinking. Throughout their school experience of mathematics children can use patterns to establish connections within mathematics and to relate mathematics to the world around them. The disposition to find patterns — to search for regularity and similarity among different phenomena — is helpful in approaching any new area of investigation.

Challenges in this set are intended only as samples. When your students have seen a few such examples, they will probably come up with many more interesting ones of their own. If students find it difficult to draw or state the next entry in a pattern, it might help them to have some possible answers shown from which one can be selected, placed, and verified. Make sure that students realize that some do not have "correct answers." What is most important is the reasoning behind the selection of the next element.

Most of these patterns are visual, or the numbers can be related to visual images. You may find that different children excel with visual patterning challenges than with more numerical ones. Some challenges have more than one part. You might try showing the first part of the problem for a day or so before adding the second part, which is a visual hint. Or try the two parts in the reverse order.

Most patterns in this set are special types of functions, or rules that associate another number or shape to each of the numbers 1, 2, 3, ... (the position in the sequence, 1st, 2nd, 3rd, etc.) See Guess My Rule, Set 17, for other examples of functions. Most of these challenges can be extended by asking what is the 20th term in the sequence. Probably students will find this more difficult to answer than to predict the next few terms.

A Children should notice the double pattern, the alternation of square and triangle, and also the clockwise movement of the shaded part around the shapes. Notice that such a pattern can provide incidental practice of vocabulary for shape or fractional parts. A follow-up question is to ask how many terms there are before a shape appears that is exactly like the first one.

B Have children compare their strategies on this. Some might go row by row ("dot, slant up, slant down, dot, ...") while others might see larger elements in the pattern ("a row of diamonds that just touch"). You might have children copy this in the center of some grid paper, and figure out how to extend the pattern in all directions. (Many answers are possible.) Patterns like this can be explored with small squares of cardboard on an empty grid. Children can be asked how many different such tiles are needed to make this pattern, and to predict how many of each type will be needed if the page is to be covered. It might help to see that the 3 × 3 square below is a "building block" for the pattern, and such a block requires

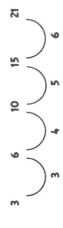

1 tile like ⊠ ,
2 tiles like ◯ ,
2 tiles like ⊡ , and
4 tiles like ◻ .

C This one may mystify many children, until you lay a strip of paper horizontally just below the pattern, and ask what is hiding. For some reason, the image of the alphabet jumps right out!

D This challenge relates addition of 5 and subtraction of 2 to movements to the right and left on the number line. First let students tackle the purely numerical pattern. Later show the number line as a hint, and also as a motivation for the question: What would come before the 1? and before that? Even if students have not yet studied negative numbers, they can consider this question and lay the intuitive groundwork for arithmetic with negatives.

E Part a of this pattern is the triangular numbers. (See Cubes, Set 6, Challenge A.) To get the next numbers, children can look at differences between successive terms in part a:

3 ⌢ 6 ⌢ 10 ⌢ 15 ⌢ 21

3, 4, 5, 6

or draw the next triangle in part b. Except for 1, the numbers in part c are all successive multiples of 3. The pattern in part c is given by the outside or black dots in the visual patterns of part b. Students might see that the triangular numbers are again appearing in the white middle part of the pattern.

F These are the dates of Sundays in 1992. Make this more up to date by using the dates of successive Sundays starting with the current month. Then, as a hint, you can place the pattern and the current calendar next to each other.

G This pattern is a code. As a hint, write the numbers 1, 2, 3, ... below each symbol and ask: Which numbers have only one symbol? (primes) Which have symbols with circles? (even numbers) Eventually, have students write the prime factorization for each number and compare it with the visual pattern given. Note that the symbol for 13 could be anything new.

H This pattern is the square numbers minus 4 (i.e. corners are removed in the diagrams.) If students are not shown the visual interpretation, they are more likely to find the next terms by noting patterns of differences:

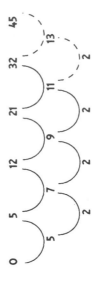

0 ⌢ 5 ⌢ 12 ⌢ 21 ⌢ 32 ⌢ 45

5 7 9 11 13

2 2 2 2

Students may note that the terms are 0 × 4, 1 × 5, 2 × 6, 3 × 7, 4 × 8. Students who have seen some algebra might be amused to recognize that these two descriptions of the same pattern verify that $n^2 - 4 = (n - 2)(n + 2)$.

CHALLENGE SET : 16

what is the question?

In each of these challenges, you are shown some information and the answer to a question, but not the question. You are to find a question that has that answer.

You do not have to use all of the information shown.

C. Missing Story

This is what I wrote to solve a story problem.

What could the story have been?

$$\begin{array}{r} 4 \\ \times 3 \\ \hline 12 \end{array} \qquad \begin{array}{r} 12 \\ + 5 \\ \hline 17 \end{array}$$

Answer: 17

F. Shapes on a Grid

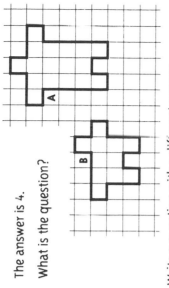

The answer is 4.

What is the question?

Write a question with a different answer.

D. Pizza

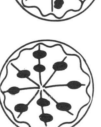

The answer is 1/8.

What is the question?

Write a question with a different answer.

G. Which Shapes?

A   B   C   D   E

The answer is only A and D.

What is the question?

Write a question with a different answer.

A. Candy

The answer is 8.

What is the question?

Write a question with a different answer.

3¢ →
2¢ →

E. Same Division, Different Answers

Write story problems that require the division $35 \div 4 = 8$ R 3 to have the following answers:

a.   8

b.   3

c.   9

d.   8.75

H. An Algebraic Equation

Here is an algebraic equation written about a story problem.

$$5N - 3 = 15$$

Write a story it would correspond to.

B. Pencils

The answer is 3.

What is the question?

15¢
13¢
25 25

Write a question with a different answer.

Much of the difficulty in solving real-life problems is in formulating the right question. This set of challenges gives students experience in finding questions for a given circumstance, or coming up with a story to match a numerical solution.

Many students have difficulty with solving story problems. Students cannot rely on memory of facts alone. They must have understanding of the concepts underlying arithmetic. Sometimes the difficulty is blamed on students' reading ability, but reading story problems aloud is not much help to most students. Perhaps the difficulty stems from formalizing arithmetic too early, and not emphasizing enough in what sort of situations it is appropriate to add, subtract, multiply or divide.

One strategy for helping students in this area is to have them write their own story problems. In the challenges in this set, specifying the answer focuses attention on certain aspects, and provides additional challenge. However, at other times in school, students should have more open experiences in writing questions for each other, deciding what is too little, enough, or too much information. Chapter 7 in Marilyn Burns' A Collection of Math Lessons From Grades 3 Through 6 describes a lesson in which children are given a situation like Challenge B but without requiring a fixed answer. This lesson indicates both the wide range of questions children will come up with, and also the amount they can learn through such question-writing experiences.

At a more complex level, students can use real life data, such as that provided on supermarket handouts, restaurant menus, timetables, rate charts for long distance telephone calls or postage, or school book order forms. (See Children's Literature, Set 3S, Challenge C, for ideas on this.)

A It should be emphasized that there are several questions with the answer 8. Examples are: "How many cents would 2 candy canes and 1 lollipop

cost?" or "How many cents would 4 lollipops cost?" or "If I spend 16¢ on lollipops, how many will I have?"

B This challenge differs from the one before by introducing the idea that there might be a certain amount of money with which one can shop. One question might be "How many of the long pencils could I buy with the 50¢?"

C A student's response to this challenge can enable a teacher to check for understanding of multiplication and addition concepts. Giving a context might help, for example, shopping or cooking. Possible questions then might be "I bought 3 books for $4 each and 1 book for $5. How much did I spend?" or "I'm making cookies for my family. Three people want 4 cookies but my big brother wants 5. How many must I make?"

D The question here might be how much pizza is left over if all children have the same number of slices, and they eat as much as possible. (Since there are 16 slices each child could get 5, leaving 1 slice left over.)

E Students often don't know what to do with the remainder and this challenge focuses on this issue. If desired, give this a context, such as the class. Here are some "natural" stories framed in this context.

There are 35 students in a class. We have a game which requires exactly 4 students to play. How many games can be played at one time in the class? (Answer is 8.)

In the situation above, how many children will not be playing? (Answer is 3.)

The 35 students in the class are going on a car trip. Four students can fit in each car. How many cars are needed? (Answer is 9.)

Each of the 35 students in the class contributes $1 to a fund to buy presents for needy children. The money is to be shared by 4 children. How much will each get? (Answer is $8.75.)

As a class project, select one story from each student, put them on cards, and challenge students to match stories to answers. (This could become a bulletin board display.)

F If you draw these on centimeter grid paper, then all questions can be phrased in terms of centimeters or square centimeters. One possible question is "What is the difference between the perimeters of figures A and B [in centimeters]?" Here are a few more possible answers, with their questions:

16 ("How many sides does A have?")
17 ("What is the area of B [in square units]?")
20 ("What is the perimeter of A?")
31 ("What is the sum of the areas of A and B?")

Some teachers hesitate to mix area and perimeter problems because students so often confuse these concepts, but that is probably a result of an overemphasis on formulas. With figures like these, students must rely on fundamental concepts, and count units.

G One question might be "Which shapes have exactly 2 lines of symmetry?" Another might be "Which have names beginning with the letter 'R'?" (although one might object that a square is a special type of rectangle). To review specific vocabulary, show a set of shapes and give a list of words, one of which must be used in the question. For this set of quadrilaterals, appropriate vocabulary words might include: right angle; opposite sides; opposite angle; congruent; adjacent.

Check that students' stories are appropriate.

H Suppose that a student writes "I had 5 times as many marbles as you but then I lost 3. Now I have 15. How many do you have?" This story is inappropriate because one cannot normally have a fraction of a marble. However, if a similar story was written about dollars, it would be appropriate. You could have different groups of students each do a similar equation, $5N + 3 = 15$, $3N + 5 = 15$, etc. Then stories could be collected, and the class challenged to match stories to expressions.

CHALLENGE SET : 17

guess my rule

In each of these challenges, there is a "rule" to be guessed.

See if you can describe the rules in more than one way.

A. Magic Box

Here is a set of cards. When you put them in the magic box, they come out as shown.

What will happen for the next cards?

6 → 3

9 → 1

3 → 6

4 → 8

8 → ?

3 → ?

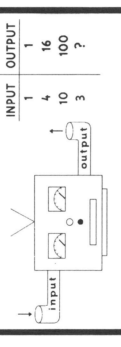

5

MAGIC BOX

in

out

2

B. Unfolding Cards

Some cards have been unfolded.

What is hidden on the folded cards?

3 6

10 20

4 8

0 8

10

2

C. Mystery Machine

You put a number into this machine and a number comes out. Here are some results.

What does the machine do?

INPUT	OUTPUT
1	1
4	16
10	100
3	?

input

output

D. Two Mystery Machines

Two machines are linked together. You put a number in the first, it does something to it and passes the result to the second. Then a number comes out of the second machine.

What could the machines be doing?

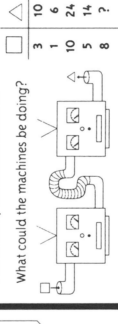

□	△
3	10
1	6
10	24
5	14
8	?

E. Diagonals

A diagonal of a polygon is a line from a vertex to a vertex which lies inside the polygon. This pentagon has 5 diagonals.

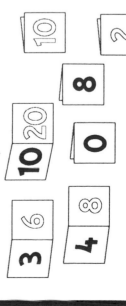

How many diagonals does a triangle have? A quadrilateral?

How many diagonals does a 20-sided figure have?

F. How High Will It Bounce?

Hold a ball at these heights, let it go, and observe how high it bounces:

40 cm, 60 cm, 80 cm, 100 cm.

Predict how high it will bounce if you release it from 70 cm.

G. The Tower of Hanoi

You will need 6 discs of different sizes, and 3 spaces to put them in. You can only move one disc at a time. A disc can be moved only to an empty space or on top of a disc that is larger than it.

What is the smallest number of moves that it would take to move the discs from the left space to the right space? (*Hint: try to answer this question using fewer discs.*)

H. How Many Factors?

4 has three factors, 1, 2 and 3.
5 has two factors, 1 and 5.
6 has four factors, 1, 2, 3 and 6.

Find ways to fill in the empty spaces in this chart.

Number	4	5	6	7	12			
Number of factors	3	2	4			1	3	5	8

The Mathematical Toolbox   © 1992 Cuisenaire Company of America, Inc.

Commentary:17
GUESS MY RULE

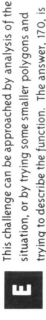

These challenges deal with functions, which are important in many branches of mathematics, although sometimes we know them by other names. A function is a rule that assigns to any element of one set an element in another set (possibly the same). The Guess My Rule format is a general one which can be applied to many mathematical topics. A few "inputs" are given together with their corresponding "outputs." Students are to guess the results of applying the function to other inputs, and to describe the function. Students can choose what inputs they want to try.

Many other challenges in this book ask students to guess a rule or describe a function. In *What Could Come Next?*, Set 15, the patterns are special types of functions, where the inputs are taken from the counting numbers 1, 2, 3, ... and outputs are diagrams or numbers. *Concept Cards*, Set 13, can also be viewed as a Guess My Rule format, where the input is the various forms, shapes, numbers, etc., and the output is "yes" or "no." Some (but not all) of the arrows in *Language of Arrows*, Set 23, represent functions (for example "+2" or "x3") and some challenges in that set are in a Guess My Rule format.

This set shows a way in which Guess My Rule can fit into a weekly classroom routine. Choice of the actual function can depend on the level of students and on topics currently under study. A few inputs and their outputs can be shown at the start of the week, with a new one added each day until students can successfully predict outputs. This procedure will work for the clever Magic Box of Challenge A, the folded cards of Challenge B, or the image of Mystery Machines in Challenges C and D. Note that these three devices can be appropriate for older students as well. Also students can make up new rules to be used in these formats. Outputs for the rules or functions of Challenges E – H can be determined through experimentation.

For a systematic development of functions for upper elementary school students, see the Madison Project materials, in particular *Discovery in Mathematics, A Text for Teachers* by Robert B. Davis. The description of features of this project starts "The Madison Project materials are founded on the belief that good mathematics is somewhat akin to good jazz – it must be **experienced**, and the **spirit** is more important than the outward form." The program develops algebraic notation and concepts, and also builds on the interplay between graphs and algebraic notation for functions. There are many opportunities for discoveries and creative thought on the part of students.

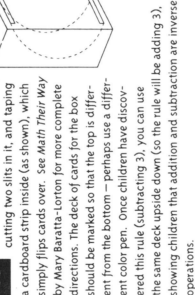

A   A Magic Box can be made from a tall box (such as a milk carton) by cutting two slits in it, and taping a cardboard strip inside (as shown), which simply flips cards over. See *Math Their Way* by Mary Baratta-Lorton for more complete directions. The deck of cards for the box should be marked so that the top is different from the bottom — perhaps use a different color pen. Once children have discovered this rule (subtracting 3), you can use the same deck upside down (so the rule will be adding 3), showing children that addition and subtraction are inverse operations.

B   Prepare these cards in two colors. (In the illustration numerals are either solid or outlined.) Cards can be held closed with paperclips, and taped or pinned to the wall. Notice that some cards are folded so that the "input" shows, and some so the "output" shows.

C   Students enjoy making a Mystery Machine from a box. For drama, use a huge box and have a child inside writing the "outputs" on slips of paper. In the example shown, the output is the square of the input.

D   When machines are linked like this, there will probably be many possible answers. In the example shown, some students may say "the first machine is adding 2 and the second is doubling" while others might say "the first is doubling and the second is adding 4." Stated algebraically, they are finding an example of the distributive property of multiplication over addition, that is, $2(\square + 2) = 2\square + 4$. Students will find that in some cases, the outputs of the linked machines are the same in either order (for example, when both machines are adding a number), while in other cases, the order makes a difference (for example, when one machine adds and the other multiplies).

E   This challenge can be approached by analysis of the situation, or by trying some smaller polygons and trying to describe the function. The answer, 170, is the same as the handshake problem but one must subtract the number of sides of the polygon, 20. (See the commentary on *Counting*, Set 21, Challenge H.)

F   This function is determined by a physical experiment. Error of measurement will probably be an issue here, and students might try, say, 5 times for each starting height, and average the results. Students might graph the results, draw a curve connecting the data, and use this to predict results.

G   This function is determined by acting out a puzzle, which in itself demands a systematic approach. It helps to see how many moves it takes to move a pile of 1 disk (1 move), 2 (3 moves), 3 (7 moves), 4 (15 moves), etc. Students might notice that these numbers are one less than the powers of 2. To move n disks it will take $2^n - 1$ moves. This puzzle is discussed in *Explorations in Mathematics* by Robert B. Davis, another book from The Madison Project.

H   Although this function is difficult to describe completely, students should be able to get some partial results. All prime numbers have 2 factors. Only square numbers have an odd number of factors. Only 1 has one factor. At some point, suggest that students find the prime factorization of each number. This may help them to find the rule: Write the number as a product of prime numbers, with exponents 1 or higher. For example $60 = 2^2 \times 3^1 \times 5^1$. Then the number of factors is found by adding 1 to each exponent and multiplying these numbers. 60 has $(2+1) \times (1+1) \times (1+1) = 12$ factors.

replacement puzzles

A numerical expression is written with some blank square spaces. In a loop are some numerals. The challenge is to arrange the numerals in the squares, using each one exactly once, so that a correct statement or consistent pattern is formed.

It may help to write the numerals on small squares of paper and experiment by moving these around.

F. Equivalent Fractions

$$\frac{\square}{\square} = \frac{\square}{\square} \qquad \frac{\square}{\square} = 1 \qquad \frac{\square}{\square} = 2$$

$$\frac{\square}{\square} = \frac{\square}{\square}$$

(numerals: 3, 6, 2, 4, 6, 3, 8, 2)

G. Two Operations

$$3 \times (\square + \square) = \frac{\square}{\square}$$

$$\square + \square = \frac{\square}{\square}$$

$$\square \times \square = \square$$

(numerals: 7, 1, 6, 3, 2, 8, 4, 5, 8)

H. Square Roots

$$\sqrt{\square\square} + \sqrt{\square} = \sqrt{\square\square} + \sqrt{\square}$$

(numerals: 0, 1, 2, 1, 5, 6)

C. Multi-digit Addition

$$
\begin{array}{ccc}
& \square & \square \\
+ & \square & \square \\
\hline
\square & \square & \square \\
\end{array}
$$

(numerals: 7, 1, 6, 3, 6, 0, 9)

D. Inequalities

$$\square + \square < \square + \square$$

$$\square + \square > \square - \square$$

(numerals: 1, 2, 6, 7, 3, 4, 8, 5)

E. Multiplication Facts

$$
\frac{\square\,\square}{\square} \times \frac{\square}{\square} \qquad \frac{\square\,\square}{\square} \times \frac{\square}{\square} \qquad \frac{\square\,\square}{\square} \times \square
$$

(numerals: 4, 1, 4, 5, 0, 2, 5, 3, 2, 8, 5)

A. Patterns

3 4 3 4 4 3 4 4

1 2 3 2 3 4 5

1 2 2 3 3 4 4 4

$$
\begin{array}{ccc}
\square & \square & \square \\
\square & \square & \square \\
\square & \square & \square \\
\end{array}
$$

(numerals: 5, 4, 4, 4, 5, 3, 6, 5, 4)

B. Addition Facts

$$\frac{\square\,\square}{\square} + \square \qquad \frac{\square\,\square}{\square} + \square \qquad \frac{\square\,\square}{\square} + \square$$

(numerals: 2, 5, 8, 5, 3, 5, 1, 3, 8, 3)

Commentary:18
REPLACEMENT PUZZLES

In the traditional mathematics curriculum, students spent much of their time in reviewing previously learned computational skills, usually depending only on memory. Students today must develop a level of computational skill appropriate for our world, yet they should at the same time be challenged to use higher order thinking skills. Replacement puzzles provide a way to combine computational practice with analysis of the algorithms being practiced. This type of challenge has several desirable features.

1. Their format is very adaptable. You or children can easily make more puzzles of this type to review or practice almost any computational skill. Simply take an exercise, and list the digits on the side. It may be hard to predict the difficulty without trying the challenge. A hint can always be provided by leaving some digits in place.

2. Most puzzles like this have more than one solution. It is interesting to compare solutions, and see if one solution suggests another. A student who finds a solution quickly can be challenged by asking how many different solutions can be found.

3. The level of difficulty of each puzzle can be adapted by giving hints. If children are stuck, you can place one or more numerals in a correct position to get them started. Students need to have some success in order to develop confidence to tackle more difficult problems. (Sometimes though, placing numerals can make a challenge more difficult, as in D.)

4. The puzzles encourage the use of higher order thinking skills. Students might approach the puzzles using only trial and error, but they will be more successful if they try to analyze the format, and think about where to start, how placement of one numeral affects another, which placements are impossible, and so forth. Strategies that might be encouraged in the specific problems are described below.

It is very helpful for students to have numerals to move around, rather than to have to erase frequently as they experiment. An easy and attractive way to present the challenges is by using a metal-backed chalkboard (or a cookie sheet) and numeral cards with a small strip of magnetic tape glued on the back. The format and a loop are drawn, and the cards are put in the loop. As hints are given, or if students wish to experiment, the cards can be moved in and out of the blank spaces.

A If desired, fill in more entries in the pattern to the left of the blanks. Children might be encouraged to look at the patterns out of order. The first is probably easiest to see. The second might be more difficult unless children see it in groups of three. So they might do better by looking at the third pattern next. This type of pattern puzzle can be made with shapes just as well as with numerals.

B Students should see that the "1" must go in the ten's place of the third addition. Encourage them to explain why. Then the only possibilities for the third sum are 5 + 8 or 8 + 5. Students should also see that for any of the sums, the top two numbers can be exchanged to get another solution (due to the Commutative Property of Addition, although don't expect young children to know it by this name). Also the first two sums can be exchanged, so this puzzle has many different solutions, including this one.

5					2				5
+ 3				+ 3				+ 8	
8				5				1 3	

C A good place to start on this one is to realize that the zero cannot go in three of the squares. Also either the two numerals in the hundred's places have to be the same (if there is no exchange in the ten's column), or the one in the sum has to be one more than the one in the addend. One can eliminate the possibility of two 6's in the hundred's places by trial and error, leaving 1 and 2, 2 and 3, or 6 and 7 for the hundred's places. One solution is 139 + 67 = 206. There are certainly others.

D This one has many solutions. To make it more challenging, try putting "1" in the first space of the top inequality, and "8" in the first space of the bottom inequality. To solve this puzzle, it helps to realize that to make a number less, you want to subtract a greater number.

E In this one the two dotted numbers give significant hints. The first product must be 2 × 4 = 8. The third could be 2 × 5 = 10 or 3 × 5 = 15 or 3 × 4 = 12. If each of these is tried, it is seen that you can only make a multiplication from the remaining numerals when the right hand product is 3 × 5 = 15. The middle one is then 4 × 5 = 20.

F In the middle expression, numerator and denominator must be the same, 2/2, 3/3 or 6/6. The third expression for 2 must be 8/4, 6/3 or 4/2. If you start with the middle equation, then do the right, you can find several solutions. For example,

$$\frac{3}{6} = \frac{4}{8} \qquad \frac{2}{2} = 1 \qquad \frac{6}{3} = 2$$

G This puzzle might encourage students to look closely at parentheses, and hence might motivate discussion of order of operations. One strategy might be to consider the two-digit multiples of 3, namely 12, 15, 18, 21, 24, 28, …, and to rule out those where the other factor cannot be written as a sum of the remaining numerals (for example 12 and 18 are ruled out this way). One solution to this one is

$$3 \times (1 + 7) = 24$$

$$5 \times 6 + 8 = 38$$

H One strategy here is to list the available one- and two-digit numbers that are perfect squares, that is 0, 1, 4, 16, 25. This leads to the solution

$$\sqrt{25} + \sqrt{0} = \sqrt{16} + \sqrt{1}$$

CHALLENGE SET : 19

switch two

In each of these challenges, something is wrong! The error can be corrected by switching exactly two of the shapes, symbols or numerals.

When you have found one way to correct the error by "switching two," try to find another way to do it.

A. Switch Two

Switch two squares to make a nicer pattern.

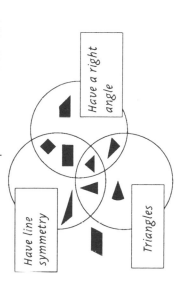

B. Switch Two

Switch two symbols to make these correct.

$$2 \quad 5$$
$$4 \quad 1$$
$$+ \quad 3 \quad 6$$
$$\overline{8 \quad 4}$$

C. Switch Two

Switch two words or shapes to make this correct.

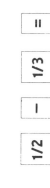

Have line symmetry — Have a right angle — Triangles

D. Switch Two

Switch two digits to make this correct.

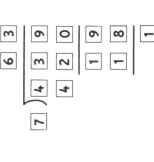

$$7 \overline{)4\ 3\ 9} \quad 6\ 3$$
$$\quad 4\ 2\ 0$$
$$\quad \overline{1\ 9} \quad 1\ 9$$
$$\quad \overline{1\ 8} \quad 1\ 8$$
$$\quad \overline{1}$$

E. Switch Two

Switch two words to make these correct.

All	rectangles	are	squares
Some	triangles	are	polygons
No	pentagons	are	trapezoids

F. Switch Two

Switch two symbols to make these correct.

1/4	>	1/6
1/2	−	1/3	=	1/5
1/8	<	1/7

G. Switch Two

Switch two symbols to make these correct.

50	%	of	20	is	10
20	%	of	8	is	10
40	%	of	20	is	50

H. Switch Two

Switch two symbols to make these correct.

2y	×	y	=	y
4y	÷	y	=	4
2y	−	2	=	4y

Commentary: 19
SWITCH TWO

These challenges ask students to correct some mathematical statements or visual displays in a particular way — by switching exactly two shapes, symbols or words. To solve some of these challenges, students must first determine which statements are true and which are false, and must then find the symbols to switch. They may find that a switch of two symbols will give a partial solution, by correcting one error but not another. Students may use a trial and error strategy for this type of challenge, but they are likely to find it time-consuming and frustrating.

Encourage students to narrow down possibilities for changes by reasoning, before trying particular switches. Challenges in this format might be useful for reviewing previously learned skills, and allow the teacher to diagnose students' levels of understanding.

These challenges are easy for you or your students to make up, in the context of whatever you are studying. They are especially easy to present on a magnetic board. Write the words, numerals or symbols on small cards on the back of which is stuck a piece of magnetic tape. When students are not in the room, arrange them on a metal-backed board (perhaps the chalkboard, or a cookie sheet) to make true statements or patterns. Then switch two of the cards. You might allow the first child to find a correct solution to do the switching for a later challenge. You can of course just draw the challenges on the board as shown, but this loses the potential for manipulation of the cards to try out different ideas.

Many challenges made in this way will have more than one solution. Encourage students who have found one solution to try to find another, if they remain interested. You can vary the format by instead switching three symbols, or changing just one.

The examples shown here are intended to suggest some of the many ways in which this format can be used to generate new challenges. For each challenge, a possible solution is shown, but others may be possible.

A

This one is nice to present on movable squares. It may seem like a lot of work to make up a set just for this challenge, but the cards can be used for many patterning experiences. (See Patchwork Quilts, Set 31, Challenge A.) Students might want to switch different squares than the ones shown. Ask children why they think one pattern is preferable. The concept of symmetry may emerge.

B

Students who approach this by trial and error may get frustrated. Encourage students to think about what must be changed. In the original, the sum is actually 102. This indicates that a digit in the tens column must be exchanged for a lesser digit in the units column. This reduces the number of switches to try.

$$\begin{array}{r} 2\ 5 \\ 4\ 3 \\ +\ 1\ 6 \\ \hline 8\ 4 \end{array}$$

C

This one is nice to adapt for a wide range of classification problems. It is best presented with cut-out shapes — be sure they are cut accurately.

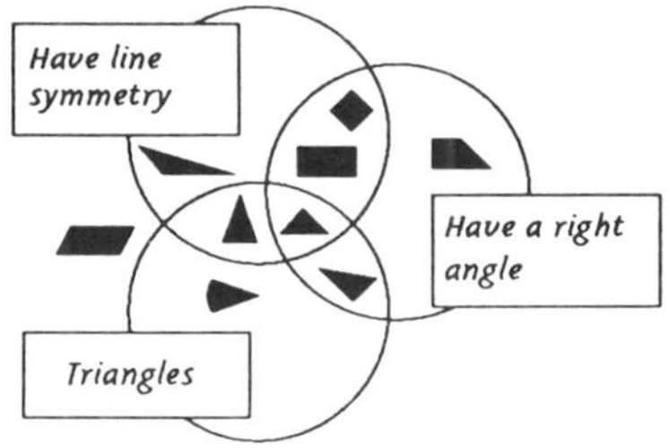

Have line symmetry
Have a right angle
Triangles

D

Students might at first note that 7 × 60 gives the first number subtracted, 420. The error appears to be that in the next step, the number subtracted is 18, not 3 × 7 = 21. This might suggest to students that an appropriate switch would be the 6 and the 7. A challenge like this encourages students to analyze steps in the algorithm for division, rather than to just practice it in a mechanical way.

$$\begin{array}{r} 7\ 3 \\ 6\ )\overline{4\ 3\ 9} \\ 4\ 2\ 0 \\ \hline 1\ 9 \\ 1\ 8 \\ \hline 1 \end{array}$$

E

The only original statement that is false is the first. The sentences could be corrected by switching "rectangles" and "squares," like this:

All	squares	are	rectangles
Some	triangles	are	polygons
No	pentagons	are	trapezoids

Students should certainly accept as true that "All squares are rectangles," yet they may be less comfortable with the statement that "Some triangles are polygons." In everyday language, when we say *some*, we may imply *some but not all*. But in mathematical usage, *some* means *some, maybe all*. And so students may be more comfortable with this solution:

Some	rectangles	are	squares
All	triangles	are	polygons
No	pentagons	are	trapezoids

F

Students might question what a "symbol" means in this problem. Can they switch an entire fraction? If the challenge is presented on movable cards, it is clear what can be switched. Let students determine the rules. The solution shown uses the more stringent requirement that only a single digit counts as a symbol. This challenge, like E, requires a switch of a symbol in a statement that is already correct.

1/4	>	1/5
1/2	–	1/3	=	1/6
1/8	<	1/7

G

Students should realize that since the second and third statements are false, a number in one must be switched with another.

50	% of	20	is	10
20	% of	50	is	10
40	% of	20	is	8

H

This one requires switching symbols for operations.

2y	–	y	=	y
4y	÷	y	=	4
2y	×	2	=	4y

CHALLENGE SET : 20

estimation

These challenges involve estimation. Estimation is an important aspect of using mathematics in a wide variety of situations. Often an estimate is more useful than an exact count.

Think of something else that would be interesting to estimate.

A. Comparing

Which container will hold more raisins?

(Shown is a snack-size raisin box and a coffee scoop, but you can use other containers.)

B. Cubes in a Jar

Which color has more?

(This requires a jar with a mixture of two colors of cubes. You could also use other objects, such as marbles, nuts, macaroni.)

C. Scoopfuls of Beans

About how many kidney beans will fit in the coffee scoop?

D. Loops and Dots

There are 20 dots in the loop. How many dots are there in all?

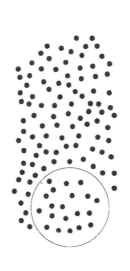

E. Counting

How long would it take you to count aloud from one to one million?

999,998, 999,999, 1,000,000 — Ready or not, here I come!

F. Colored Toothpicks

Estimate the percentages of the toothpicks in this box which are of each color.

Party Pics 250

G. "A Picture is Worth 1000 Words"

Find a picture in the newspaper which is "worth 1000 words," that is, which takes up as much space as 1000 words.

H. Popcorn—Before and After

Before: Estimate how many kernels of popcorn are in the jar.

After: Estimate by what percent the volume will increase when the corn is popped.

Before: Estimate the weight of the kernels of popcorn are in the jar.

After: Estimate by what percent the weight will increase or decrease when the corn is popped.

In many of our everyday uses of mathematics an estimate is more important than an exact count. All work with number is richer for students who have a good "number sense" — a feeling for about how many or how large things are. Estimation is also very helpful in computation, in particular when one uses a calculator, so that one can catch obvious errors.

This challenge set shows varied contexts and strategies for estimation of number. (Strategies for exact counting are explored in Counting, Set 11.) Estimation appears in many other challenge sets, in particular in the ones on measurement.

In the Curriculum and Evaluation Standards for School Mathematics proposed by the National Council of Teachers of Mathematics it is suggested that

"The class is given the opportunity to plan and participate in an all-school "Estimation Day." The children, in pairs or threes, are to design estimation activities to be completed by children in other classes. Each group will supply all the necessary materials and monitor the activities. The activities might include guessing children's heights, the number of candies in a jar, the lengths of various pieces of string, the weight of a bag of potatoes, the length of the room, the number of times they can write their names in a minute, or the length of time required for an ice cube to melt."

This experience might follow exposure to some of the challenges in this set. Children might also set up such activities for parents at a PTA meeting.

An estimation jar can be used as an ongoing weekly activity. Find several jars which are uniform in size, and each week fill one with some common object. Each student puts an estimate in a guess box. At the end of the week, the estimates can be ordered, grouped, graphed, and averaged (depending on skills of the students). When the objects are counted, the jar should be labeled with the number, and left out to compare with the next jar, filled with different objects.

The 1986 yearbook of the National Council of Teachers of Mathematics, Estimation and Mental Computation, is an excellent resource on this topic.

A If you set up the containers to be compared in front of a magnetic chalkboard, have children place their nametags (with a small piece of magnetic tape on the back) above their choice. This gives experience in making a bar graph, and at the same time helps you to take attendance. Try to find two containers where the difference in capacity is not perceptually obvious. Instead of raisins, you can use other small objects.

B Ask children how they decided. They may "eyeball" it — or they may count what they can see and predict what is out of sight. The answer can be checked by sorting the contents and matching the two sets. It could be an interesting extension to use two objects of different sizes, such as walnuts and acorns.

C Ask students how they estimated. They may first estimate how many beans just cover the bottom of the scoop. When they count the beans, give a scoopful to each of several pairs of children. Have them count groups of ten into an egg carton. Will all the counts be the same? Why not? What is the average? As a follow-up, repeat with different types of beans.

D This challenge suggests a strategy for estimating — comparing to a "benchmark" or known quantity. If you draw lots of dots on a chalkboard or large sheet of paper, have students make an exact count at the end of the week by looping all dots in groups of 10 or 20. Later try a similar estimation challenge without providing this strategy, and see if students think of it.

E Students might time themselves as they read aloud a list of some six-digit numbers. It takes about 2 seconds to say each of these, and so it would take

2 million seconds to count to 1 million. Divide by 60 to get minutes, then by 60 to get hours, then by 24 to get days, and the result is about 23 days. This and many other ways to estimate large numbers are presented in *How Much Is a Million?* by David M. Schwartz, delightfully illustrated by Steven Kellogg.

F Present this challenge with a box of the fancy colored "party pics" which come in boxes of 250. If you use wooden toothpicks, you can follow this estimation challenge with an experiment — take the box of toothpicks out to a grassy area and toss them all over the grass. Then give the class 5 minutes to find as many as they can. Have them calculate the percentages of each color when the toothpicks are gathered again. They will probably find that the percentage of green has decreased, because the green blends into the grass, thus demonstrating the value of camouflage. (Plastic toothpicks should not be used for this experiment because any which are not found will not decompose.)

A similar challenge could be posed using any other small items that come in mixed colors.

G This challenge can be approached through area. Students can count how many words are in, say a strip 2 x 5 cm long, and then find the area of a strip with 1000 words. Answers will depend on the size of the newspaper print.

H Encourage students to find ways to estimate the number of kernels without counting more than, say, 30 kernels. They might do this by weight (weighing 30 kernels, and then weighing all of them), or by capacity (counting how many fit in a spoon, how many spoons fill a scoop, and how many scoops fill the jar), or even by area (spread kernels evenly into a rectangle on centimeter grid paper and count how many fit in, say, 4 square centimeters). An estimate of the percentage increase in volume might depend on the age and quality of the popcorn — just how many "dead" kernels does one expect? Students are often surprised that the weight stays almost the same. A tiny bit of steam escapes when a kernel pops, but also a tiny bit of salt or butter may be added. This activity gives experience with the idea of density.

CHALLENGE SET : 21

counting

These challenges all require some sort of an exact count. You will probably find that you will need some strategies for counting, other than just "one, two, three ..." You may need to organize how you count, or look for patterns.

A. Comparing

Which are there more of in the classroom, chairs or people?

Which are there more of in the classroom, tables or people?

What has the *same* number as the number of people in the room?

B. Hidden Shapes

How many triangles are there?

C. Grouping

How many little squares (like ▢) are in this figure?

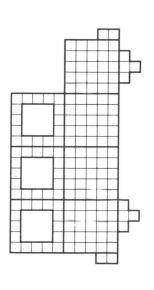

D. Legs

How many legs are in the classroom?

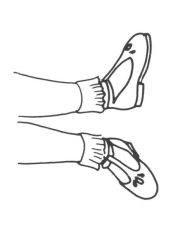

E. Special for P.S. 169

How many numbers less than 1000 can be written using only 1's, 6's and 9's as digits?

111   16   9   61   61

F. Squares

How many squares are in this diagram?

(There are more than 25!)

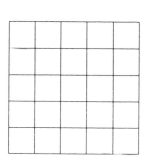

G. City Streets

How many different routes can you take from point A to point B on this map, always traveling the shortest distance possible?

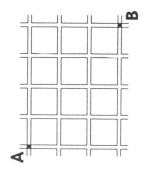

A
B

H. Handshakes

At a meeting of 20 people, each person shakes hands exactly once with every other person present. How many handshakes occur?

These challenges call for exact counts (unlike those in Estimation, Set 20), and suggest varied strategies, such as counting by groups, organizing things to be counted, using the counting principle, and looking for patterns.

Children should not be pushed to count before they are ready, but once they have started, they often enjoy counting enormously and can't be stopped. Some young children become fanatic counters; counting steps they climb, bites they eat, crayons in the crayon box, books on the bookshelf. This counting eventually becomes boring unless the challenges increase and suggest new strategies and techniques.

In the discussion of each challenge below, first are given some questions that you might ask after a while to clarify the original question.

A "Can everyone sit down at the same time? Can everyone have their own table? Are there more chairs or tables? Children or paintbrushes? legs or shoes? What are some other things where we have more (or less) than the number of people in the class?" Even before you might expect counting, you can use these challenges as an opportunity to notice if counting is attempted by individual children. Focus on resolving the issues by matching.

B "Do you see some "upside-down" triangles? Do you see triangles of different sizes? Do you count if you classify the triangles into these types, making a total of 13:

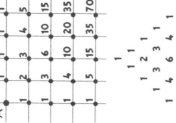

You can simplify or extend this pattern. Children might draw some of their own patterns and challenge others to find all of a given shape. Children may not be able to draw

---

very accurately. Consider letting them make patterns on a geoboard for this activity, then possibly transferring their pattern to geoboard dot paper.

C "Why are some of the grid lines darker?" To count this accurately, it is useful to see the structure of fives and tens which is embedded in the graph paper. Students can group by 5's, 10's, 25's or 100's. They can make up challenges like these themselves by drawing on graph paper with these subdivisions marked.

D "What has legs, besides people? Do we have any animals in the classroom? What about the furniture?" Children will need to systematically figure out how many 2-legged, 4-legged animals or objects there are. They will need to consider tables and chairs. Some might wonder if there are any spiders or other insects.

E "Could you write 1? 66? 911?" Students will need to plan a systematic way to count. They might organize their counting by the number of digits.

There are 3 1-digit numbers. There are 3 "doubles" (11, 66, 99) in the 2-digit numbers and 6 others which can be organized as pairs (16 and 61, 19 and 91, 69 and 96), for a total of 9. For the 3-digit numbers, there are 3 "triples," and 6 with all 3 digits (can you find them?); to count the others, find all ways of having 2 digits the same and one different, of which there are 6 (116, 661, 119, 991, 669, 996). Each of these combinations yields 3 arrangements, that is 116 yields 116, 161, and 611, and so there are 3 × 6 = 18 numbers with exactly 2 digits the same, making 3 + 6 + 18 = 27 3-digit numbers. The final answer would be 3 + 9 + 27 = 39.

Perhaps some students, familiar with the counting principle, would see that there are 9 2-digit numbers because you have 3 choices for the first digit and 3 independent choices for the second digit, making 3 × 3 possible numbers. The same reasoning shows that there are 3 × 3 × 3 = 27 possible 3-digit numbers. The second type of reasoning is more "elegant," but students might need to experience the first, more direct counting approach to appreciate the elegance. As an extension, ask how the problem would be different for, say, P.S. 230 or P.S. 177.

F "Do you see more than 26?" Note that squares can be of any size. There is a pattern. There are clearly 25 1 x 1's and 16 2 x 2's and 9 3 x 3's. Careful counting shows that there are 4 4 x 4's and 9 3 x 3's. If students examine the numbers 1, 4, 9, ___, 25, they will probably see that these are square numbers. They can count to verify that there are 16 2 x 2 squares. Try the same challenge with different-sized rectangles made up of squares. Or ask how many rectangles there are in this diagram.

G "In how many ways can you get here?" It helps if students try to find out how many ways they can get from A to each point of the grid. A pattern emerges. You get the number for an intersection by adding the numbers at the intersections above and to the left. This problem leads to an example of Pascal's Triangle.

A					
1	1	1	1	1	1
1	2	3	4	5	
1	3	6	10	15	
1	4	10	20	35	
1	5	15	35	70	

$$\begin{array}{cccc} & & 1 & \\ & 1 & & 1 \\ 1 & & 2 & & 1 \\ 1 & 3 & & 3 & 1 \\ 1 & 4 & 6 & 4 & 1 \end{array}$$

H "What if there were only a few people in the room? 2? 3?" Again, a pattern will emerge. This is fun to do if you have different-sized groups of students to act it out. Students may think of many different strategies. Some might draw a visual representation (dots are people, lines are handshakes). Some might plan an organized way to act out the problem (the first person shakes hands with 19 others and then is finished, now another person shakes hands with the 18 others left, and then is finished. If you keep going, you will have 190 = 19 + 18 + 17 + ... + 3 + 2 + 1 handshakes.) Others might reason that every one of the 20 shakes hands with 19 others, and so they multiply 20 by 19 and then divide by 2 because each handshake was counted twice. This problem leads to the triangular numbers (1, 3, 6, 10, 15, ...) which are actually embedded in Pascal's Triangle. (Also see Cubes, Set 6, Challenges A and E.)

2 people,
1 handshake

3 people,
3 handshakes

4 people,
6 handshakes

5 people,
10 handshakes

CHALLENGE SET : 22

graphing

These challenges all show graphs, but there are no labels to show what they are about. You are to think of labels so that the graph would be an accurate description of students in your class, grade or school.

To get ideas, look at how graphs are used in magazines or newspapers.

A. Label the Graph

What information about people in this room would fit the description below?

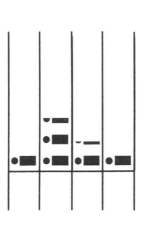

B. Label the Graph

What information about people in this room would fit the description below?

C. Label the Graph

What information about people in this room would fit the description below?

D. Label the Graph

What information about people in this room would fit the description below?

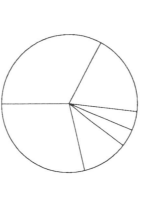

E. Label the Graph

What information about people in your grade would fit the description below?

F. Label the Graph

What information about people in your grade would fit the description below?

G. Label the Graph

What information about people in this school would fit the description below?

H. Label the Graph

What information about people in this school would fit the description below?

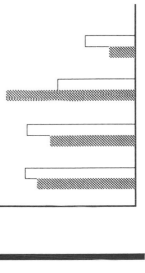

Commentary: 22
GRAPHING

One of the most frequently seen uses of mathematics in other curriculum areas, and in the current media, is in the visual representation of data in graphs. As the saying goes, at all levels a graph (which is a type of picture) can be worth a thousand words.

Graphing may be perceived by students as a straightforward matter of counting and recording given data, involving little choice. But there are many choices about how data can be represented graphically. If students spend a week collecting graphs from magazines and newspapers, they may well find examples of all the types of graphs shown in this challenge set. Different ways of presenting a given set of data highlight different aspects of the data. By thinking about the graphs in this challenge set, students might be encouraged to decide what types of data best fit these formats, and to find ways to collect data to support their ideas. It is important to find situations where students themselves figure out what data to collect, and how to represent their data.

The contexts for the graphs in this challenge set move from the classroom in the early grades, to the grade level, to the school. Of course you can adapt these contexts if appropriate. The graphs should be about contexts where students can actually collect data.

Teachers often use gender as a way to classify students. This is straightforward and the students all know where everyone fits. But one might argue that an over-emphasis on gender classification in school sends a subtle message to students that gender is important to the teacher and for school performance — a message that we certainly don't want to be extrapolated, say, to girls' performance in math and science. Try to think of other attributes of students to graph.

Another way to use the idea behind these problems is to save some old graphs made by your students, and a few months later show them — with labels removed — and challenge them to reconstruct what the graphs showed.

A The earliest forms of graphing should involve concrete objects, for example, sorting objects (shoes worn by students, vegetables used in making soup, types of acorns and nuts collected on a fall walk, . . .), and then arranging them on a grid to show relative quantity in each set. However, these types of graphs are by nature very specific, and thus will not fit the format of this challenge set where children are to find an interpretation. This graph is a bit more abstract, where a clothespin is representing something else.

You might want to present this challenge physically, using the same number of clothespins as children in the class. Some teachers use clothespins with children's names on them for attendance or classroom organization. In this case, this problem will seem natural and children will need to think of some characteristic of their classmates which divides the class into this proportion.

B This bar graph may fit an opinion poll. The challenge is to find something that about half of the students prefer. In many classes the graph may represent how students prefer to get to school (car, bus, foot or bicycle?).

C For this graph children might need to first establish how many students each little figure represents. If the class has about 30 students, each little figure might represent five students. Once these numbers are established, students might reason as in Challenge B.

D Circle graphs are useful for representing how a whole is broken down into parts. The whole might be 24 hours, the school day, the number of students in the class. So the circle graph might be personal (how an individual student spends time each day), or about class activity (how the class spends its time) or describing relative size of a subdivision of the class into six categories (favorite book, number of siblings) Students should be led to estimate how much of the whole each part represents — that is, the largest part is about one-third, the next about one-quarter, etc.

E This double bar graph could apply to situations where there are two pieces of data to be collected four times or about four things. A possible interpretation is the number of tickets to a school performance sold by 4 classes in 2 weeks. (In this case, have students try to interpret the changes. For example, perhaps the third group was too satisfied by its good performance the first week and slacked off during the second week.) Or the graph could represent the results of an opinion poll about students' preferred book to read taken in two classes.

F A broken line graph such as this should be used when there is an assumption of continuity or pattern in the data collected. The horizontal axis could be time, and the graph might represent the number of students who keep a book out of the library for a given number of days. Or the horizontal axis could be grade level, and the vertical axis the percentage of students at that grade level who watch a particular television program. This type of graph is inappropriate for representing discrete, unordered data, such as favorite flavor of ice cream.

G To find an interpretation of this graph, students must think of two different sets of data to be collected which are related in some way. Since the graph contains two broken line graphs, the data involved should be continuous (as in Challenge F above). Students might think of this graph as representing average percentages scored by students on two types of weekly tests — one of learnable skills (e.g. mastery of multiplication facts) and one of some performance which is not learnable (or perhaps, just not taught) such as musical pitch discrimination, visual memory, or fine motor coordination.

H In a graph of this sort, each dot might represent a student, and the location of the dot is determined by two different pieces of numerical information about the student. In this example, as one number increases, the other tends to also. Examples which would fit this pattern might be a students' age versus size, or height versus weight.

language of arrows

These challenges are stated in a special language. Dots represent numbers, and arrows represent relations between numbers (being greater than, a certain amount more or less than, double, ...). You might have to figure out what the dots are, or what the arrows are, or how to draw a path of dots and arrows to get from one number to another. In each challenge, all arrows of the same type represent the same relation.

A. What Does the Arrow Mean?

Label the rest of the dots.

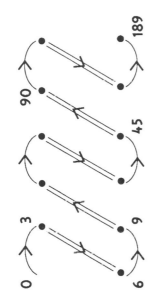

B. Draw a Path From 0 to 27

Use these arrows.

+2   +5

27

O   •

What is the greatest number of arrows you can use? the least?

Could you use just 9? just 10?

C. Label the Dots and Arrows

0   3   90   189

6   9   45

Continue the pattern.

D. Label the Dots

Use the numbers in the loop to label the dots.

➤ means "I am more than you."

19   30
27   22

E. Label the Dots

Use the numbers in the loop to label the dots.

➤ means " × ½ ="

20   100   10
24   80   12
48   40   50

F. A Number in Both Strips

⇉ means +3

➤ means +4

What numbers lie in both of the strips below?

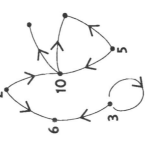

8

13

G. More Labels

What does this arrow mean?

Label the dots.

Put in a dot for 1.

Fill in some missing arrows.

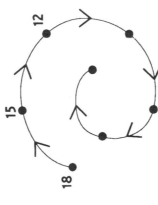

2   10   5
6   3

H. What Are the Arrows?

What could these arrows be?

Find at least two answers.

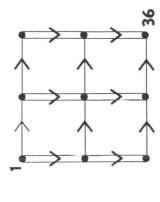

1   36

The "language of arrows" is a versatile one for expressing interesting arithmetic challenges. Students will probably be able to figure out how this language works by looking at a few examples. The arrows represent relations – for example, "is more than" or "is a factor of." Sometimes arrows are based on an arithmetic operation such as "+ 2" or "× 3." For example, if the arrow → *represents "+ 2" you could write these:*

1 → 3   6 → 4 → 4   10 → 12 → 14

but you could not write these:

2 → 6   4 → 2   6. ⟳

If you have colored chalk and are presenting the problems on a chalkboard, you can use color to distinguish the types of arrows, rather than single and double lines, as done here.

Most of the challenges below can serve as models for ones that students might write for each other.

The Comprehensive School Mathematics Program for elementary school, developed by CEMREL in the 1970's, used this language extensively (together with a "language of loops" corresponding to Venn diagrams) to pose interesting problems. Many more problems similar in the style of the ones below can be found in that program.

A The arrow means "is 3 more than." One might also read it as "is 3 more than." Students might try to extend the path in both directions. (To go from 18 back to 21, students will be using the fact that addition and subtraction are inverse operations. If they try to go beyond 0, they may invent some equivalent of the negative number –3.) If students enjoy this one, you can provide an additional challenge by making an addition chain such as this, but labeling only two points, which are not adjacent.

B Many answers are possible for this problem. The greatest number of arrows that can be used is 12

(using as many "+ 2's" as possible, which is 11, and one "+ 5"). The least is 6 (using as many "+ 5's" as possible, which is 5, and one "+ 2"). To use 9 arrows, use 3 "+ 5's" and 6 "+ 2's". You cannot use exactly 10, which can be seen by simply trying different numbers of "+ 5's." Students might notice that the order in which the arrows are written does not make a difference in the final result when both arrows are addition or subtraction of a number.

C The arrows are "+ 3" and "× 2." This puzzle can be extended by asking students to find a path using just these arrows from, say, 0 to 27, as in Challenge B. In this situation they will find that the order in which the arrows are written does make a difference.

+3 ● → ● → ●
       ×2

gives a different result from

+3 ● → ● → ●
       ×2

D This puzzle has only one solution. The dot that all the arrows are pointing to must be the least number, and the one all the arrows are pointing away from must be the greatest. The vertical arrow determines position of the other two numbers. Try having students make diagrams like this for five or six numbers, then erase the numbers and have other students try to replace the labels for the dots. (For five numbers they will get the nice pentagonal pattern shown.)

E Again there is only one answer. It is probably easiest to start with the bottom chain of 4, which must start with 80, because no other number has its half, and half again, and half again, in the loop. Students can make up more puzzles like this easily.

F Students might find the solution 5 by simply labeling a few dots in each direction. They may also

find 17 = 5 + 12 and 29 = 5 + (2 × 12). From this they may generalize that 5 more than any multiple of 12 will be on both strips. If the strips are extended to the left, they will also find –7 = 5 + (–1 × 12) on both strips, and so forth. The number 12 plays this role because it is the least common multiple of 3 and 4. To extend the challenge, give students a similar problem where arrows represent "+ 4" and "+ 6" or "+ 10" and "+ 15."

G The arrow could be "is a factor of." (It could also be "is less than or equal to.") If the dot for 1 is drawn, then it could be connected to all of the other numbers drawn (since 1 is a factor of every whole number). Also, if all loops were drawn in, there should be an arrow going from each number to itself (since each number is a factor of itself). The language of loops allows a striking visual representation of these properties of factors.

H One possibility for the arrows is "+ 10" and "+ 7.5." Another is "× 2" and "× 3." There are many other solutions where both arrows represent multiplications, or where both represent additions. It is more difficult to find a combination of addition and multiplication, because the existence of the arrow square means that the answer must be the same when you first add then multiply as when you first multiply and then add. Stated algebraically, this means that if the addition is "+ a" and the multiplication is "× b,"

$(b × 1) + a = b × (a + 1)$, or
$b + a = b × a + b$,

which means that
$a = a × b$.

This can only happen if a = 0 or if b = 1. Thus two possibilities for the arrows that combine multiplication and addition are "+ 0" and "× 6," or "+ 7.5" and "× 1." These are not satisfactory solutions, however, because one ends up with two dots in the same diagram representing the same number.

CHALLENGE SET : 24

measurement

There are many ways in which we can measure the world around us, and many reasons to measure.

As you try these challenges, think of other ways in which you use the same types of measurement.

F. Footprints

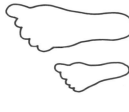

a. Trace your footprint on centimeter grid paper. Estimate the perimeter and the area of your footprint.

b. What would be the perimeter and the area of a footprint which is twice as long as yours?

G. Books

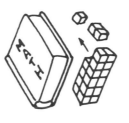

a. How many centimeter cubes would it take to make a solid the size of your math book?

b. Which takes up more space, your math book or a grapefruit? How can you tell?

H. The Earth

a. Measure the diameter and circumference of three different circles. How are the numbers related?

b. A loop of string is stretched around the equator of the earth, just touching the surface. Suppose you cut it and insert a length of string. If the string rises to the same distance from the earth all around, how much string is inserted to raise the string 1 m?

C. String

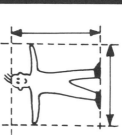

a. Cut a piece of string that just fits around your waist. Estimate how many centimeters long it is.

b. How many times will the piece of string wind around your neck? Your wrist? Your index finger?

D. Coins

a. Estimate how many pennies weigh 100 grams.

b. Which would you rather have, your weight in pennies or your height in dimes?

E. Bodies

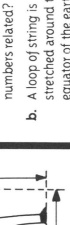

a. Which is longer, your armspan, or your height — or are they just the same?

(In other words, are you a square, a short rectangle, or a tall rectangle?)

b. In your class, which of these three types is the most common?

A. Milk Cartons

a. Estimate how many paper cups full of water will fill up the smaller carton.

b. How many will fill up the larger?

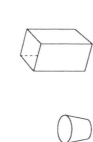

B. Paper Clips

a. Find something as long as a chain of 10 small paper clips. Estimate how many small paper clips it would take to make a chain to go the length of the room.

b. How many of the larger paper clips would it take to make a chain to go the length of the room?

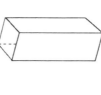

Commentary: 24
MEASUREMENT

These challenges are about measurement — of capacity, length, weight, area and volume. The problems are consistent with the approach to learning measurement advocated by the Curriculum and Evaluation Standards for School Mathematics proposed by NCTM: "The first step ... is understanding an object's many measurable attributes, such as those illustrated by a cereal box ... How much does it hold? (capacity). How tall is it? (length). How large is the front? (area). How heavy is it? (weight). How far around is the border? (length or perimeter)." In early measurement activities, children should "make decisions about the sizes of objects by looking, feeling or comparing objects directly," and thus in a natural way, build measurement vocabulary. Later, children should select and use an appropriate unit of measure, preferably directly applying the units.

As stated in the NCTM Standards, "If children's initial explorations use non-standard units, they will develop some understandings about units and come to recognize the necessity of standard units in order to communicate." (An amusing story book which expands on this theme in the context of length measurement is Rolf Myllar's How Big Is A Foot? An apprentice carpenter comes to grief when he makes a bed for the queen using his own small foot as a unit, when the queen's dimensions were measured using the king's larger foot.) Again from the Standards, "Premature use of instruments or formulas leaves children without the understanding necessary for solving measurement problems." Students should experience counting square units for area and building solids from cubes before using the related formulas.

It is also recommended that estimation be emphasized in the teaching of measurement, and that measurement skills be integrated throughout mathematics and other curriculum areas. Measurement plays a significant role in several other challenge sets, including most of those on themes or on manipulative materials. A separate set is devoted to measurement of time.

The challenges all come in two parts. In the first, students are encouraged to build their "measurement sense" by estimating and then physically measuring. In the second, direct physical measurement is used to solve a problem, find a pattern, or relate to a new measuring technique or another area of mathematics.

As always, extend and adapt these challenges to the here and now, to materials at hand and current interests.

A You can use any small container as the unit here, perhaps a coffee scoop, or a very small plastic cup. Cut-off quart and half-gallon milk cartons make suitable containers to measure. You could use the same type of carton and cut one to one-half or one-third of the height of the other. You might cover them with a solid color of Contac paper to de-emphasize the standard units of quart and gallon. You could repeat the challenge with a different sized cup as a unit.

B This challenge nicely reinforces children's study of place value (tens and ones). Children can use the object which is as long as 10 paper clips to measure across the room. If instead you want to practice, say, counting by fives, use a chain as long as 5 paper clips in part a. Part b provides an informal experience with ratio. It depends on the paper clips used, but sometimes 2 of the large ones are as long as 3 of the small ones, so 4 large ones are as long as 6 small ones, etc.

C Students sometimes guess wrongly that the length around a cylinder will be about twice the distance across (and that a string that will go around the waist is about twice the distance across). It is closer to three times — see comments on Challenge H. Ask children if their answers to part b are about the same, even if answers to part a are different. It would be interesting to compare results for a large child or adult with those for a small child.

D A penny actually weighs about 3 grams, which is useful to know if you are short of metric weights. This problem suggests a good way to measure

E This makes a nice graph. If students are interested, they might extend the question by investigating the ratio of height of body to height of head. In classical proportions, the head is meant to be one-sixth of the total height. How does the class match up? Does this proportion depend on age? (It is clearly different for babies, whose heads are larger in proportion to their bodies.)

F It may surprise students that when length doubles, the perimeter also doubles but area quadruples. Students can use string to measure around the footprint. To estimate area, they should count square centimeters inside the footprint, and decide on a strategy to deal with partially included squares (perhaps only count those more than half in the footprint, or take one-half of the total of squares which are partially in the footprint).

G An image such as that developed in part a gives meaning to the formula for volume, and should be experienced by any students who are prone to memorizing formulas without understanding them. Students may come up with various approaches to part b. They might assume that the grapefruit was approximately spherical, and apply a formula learned from a book. Encourage them to verify this result by measuring the grapefruit by displacement, that is, but immersing it in water and measuring the water displaced.

H Circumference is about 3 times diameter. (To be precise, the multiplier is π which is a little more than 3.) Students can discover and be convinced of this, by actually measuring several circles. For part b, suppose that the string around the equator has length C meters. The diameter of this circle is $D = C/\pi$. If the string is increased by π meters, it will form a circle of circumference $C + \pi$ whose diameter is $(C + \pi)/\pi = C/\pi + 1$. Increasing the string's length by 3 m yields an increase of about 1 m in diameter. This surprises most people.

CHALLENGE SET : 25

fractions

A fraction is a way in which we describe parts of things. There are many ways to visualize fractions. Do you "see" 3/4 as any of the following?

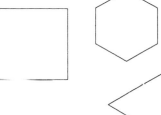

A. A Concept Card

These are blips:

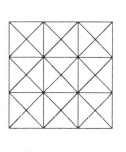

These are not blips:

Which of these are blips?

Draw something which is a blip, and something which is not a blip. What is a blip?

B. Sharing Sandwiches

Six friends have four sandwiches to share.

How should they cut them so that each gets the same amount?

How much will each friend get?

C. Congruent Parts

Cut these shapes into congruent parts to show halves, thirds, quarters, sixths and eighths.

Can you cut them into congruent parts to show other fractions?

D. A Pattern to Color

Color this square so that one-half is red, one-third is green, and the rest is yellow.

Each triangle should be just one color. Make a pattern you like.

How much of the square is yellow?

E. How Many?

The square and the circle can be filled in with numbers 1 to 6.

How many different fractions can you make?

How many different rational numbers can you make?

How many of the numbers are less than 1?

F. Danny's Pattern

Danny says: "A quarter and a third of a quarter is a third."

Then Danny says: "A fifth and a quarter of a fifth is a ....."

How did Danny finish the sentence?

Why is it true?

Write another sentence that fits this pattern.

G. Fill in the Blanks

Use the numbers in the loop to fill in the blanks. (Each can be used only once.)

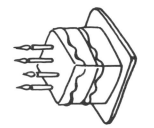

$$\frac{\square}{\square} \times \frac{\square}{\square} - \frac{\square}{\square}$$

Make the expression

a. with the greatest possible value;
b. with the least possible value.

H. Cutting the Cake

Katy has a cubical cake, frosted on the top and on four sides.

How can it be cut so that she and each of her eight friends gets exactly one-ninth of the frosting?

Commentary: 25
FRACTIONS

These challenges show thought-provoking questions can be asked about fractions at all levels. In some cases, fraction situations are introduced earlier than the grade level at which the skill is usually "covered." Students can often invent their own ways of approaching such new situations, and benefit from such experiences before being taught the standard algorithms.

A This Concept Card is intended to encourage children to verbalize the meaning of "one-third" of a region being shaded. The region must be divided into three parts which are "the same," meaning "congruent" at this level. (Later, one might expect the language "having the same area.") It is important for children to focus on both parts of this definition. It is surprising how many children will identify the shaded region to the right as "one-third." (See Concept Cards, Set 13, for discussion of this format.)

B This problem can be acted out with paper squares to represent the sandwiches. A "real life" solution might be to cut the first 3 sandwiches into 1/2s and give each friend a 1/2, and then to cut the remaining sandwich into 1/6s and share these — thus each friend gets a 1/2 and a 1/6. Some students might cut each sandwich into 6 pieces, and give a 1/6 of each sandwich to each friend, and so each friend gets 4/6s. Still others might cut each sandwich into 1/3s, giving 12/3s, so that each friend gets 2/3s. It is interesting to ask children how they might verify that the 3 solutions give the same amount of sandwich to each friend. This sort of realistic problem involving fractions can be solved by children long before they are taught the symbolic manipulations for simplifying 1/2 + 1/6 or 4/6, and will lay valuable intuitive groundwork for this later study. Chapter 3 in *A Collection of Math Lessons From Grades 3 Through 6* by Marilyn Burns describes a lesson based on this idea.

C There are many ways to cut the square into congruent halves and quarters. One way that can be generalized to all fractions is to draw equally spaced lines parallel to one edge. The triangle and hexagon are trickier. It helps to have pattern blocks available for children to manipulate. Here are some solutions.

D Students will find that there are 36 congruent small triangles, and so if the square is colored as directed, 18/36 will be red, 12/36 will be green, and the remaining 6/36 (or 1/6) will be yellow. To make the problem more challenging, ask students to form a pattern with a certain type of symmetry. (See Patchwork Quilts, Set 31, Challenge D.)

E To investigate these questions, it will help students to form an array showing all possible fractions with 1 through 6 in both numerator and denominator. (See the array in the next column.) There are 6 x 6 = 36 such fractions. However, some are equivalent. Students can go through the array and cross out all fractions that are not in lowest terms, as shown. There remain 23 different rational numbers. Finally, those less than 1 are below the diagonal. These 11 fractions are circled.

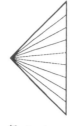

F This interesting pattern was discovered in a pizza parlor by a third grader. He explained it by saying "If you cut a pie in quarters and want to share it among 3 people, each gets one-quarter and a third of the remaining quarter." Later he explained it a different way, by saying "Well, take the quarter and a third of a quarter 3 times over, and you get a whole." Similar arguments work for any number.

G To find the largest possible value of the expression, students will need to think about the effects of changing various parts of the expression. For example, the fraction subtracted should be as small as possible and the product of the numerators of the first 2 fractions as large as possible. Students might experiment and verify results on a calculator, which may lead them to use the memory function. Solutions are as follows:

$$\frac{6}{1} \times \frac{5}{2} - \frac{3}{4} = 14\frac{1}{4} \; ; \quad \frac{2}{4} \times \frac{3}{5} - \frac{6}{1} = 5\frac{7}{10}$$

H This problem has an elegant solution. First consider how to cut a right isosceles triangle (as shown) into 9 congruent parts. If the base is divided into 9 congruent segments, and triangles formed as shown, then all triangles have the same base and height, and hence the same area. Now if 4 such right isosceles triangles are assembled into a square, and the square is cut along every fourth line segment from center to edge, each "slice" is made up of 4 triangles with the same area. This gives the slicing of the cake. The volume of each piece will be the same, and so will the icing from the sides of the cake.

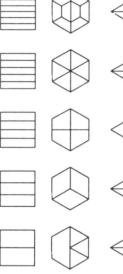

CHALLENGE SET : 26

ratio and proportion

There are many situations in everyday life where we work with the ratio between two numbers — that is, how many times one number is contained in the other, or one number divided by the other.

Most of the challenges in this set can be done without referring to ratio directly, but all have the concept underlying them.

A. Measuring With Cuisenaire Rods

My desk is 4 orange rods long.

How many yellow rods long is my desk?

B. Egg Cream Recipe

This recipe makes 4 servings of egg cream.

How much milk is needed to make 10 servings of egg cream?

Egg cream

Mix: 2 cups seltzer

3 cups milk

4 Tbs. chocolate syrup

1 tsp. of vanilla

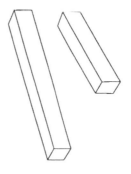

C. Oranges and Lemons

Oranges cost 5 for $1.00.

Lemons cost 8 for $1.00.

I bought 14 pieces of these fruit for $2.35.

What did I buy?

D. Weighing Cats and Dogs

5 pennies weigh as much as 3 nickels.

My dog weighs 4 times as much as my cat.

Which would you rather have, the weight of my cat in nickels or the weight of my dog in cents?

E. A Classroom Map

If the scale of a map of our classroom is 1 cm to 10 cm, draw the top of your desk, and the top of the trash can as they would appear on the map.

How large a piece of paper is needed for this map of the classroom?

F. Shadows

A woman who is 160 cm tall is standing by a tree on a sunny day.

Her shadow is 250 cm long, while the tree's shadow is 400 cm long.

How tall is the tree?

G. Chickens and Eggs

If a chicken and a half lays an egg and a half in a day and a half, how long does it take six chickens to lay a dozen eggs?

H. Two Cars Meeting

Bonnie and Clyde live 100 miles apart. They both leave their homes at noon and drive towards each other. Bonnie drives at 50 miles per hour, and Clyde drives at 30 miles per hour.

How far must Bonnie drive before they meet?

Commentary:26
RATIO AND PROPORTION

Challenges in this set concern ratio and proportion. These concepts are formalized in upper grades, but children can certainly experience them in an informal, concrete way in earlier grades. Ratio arises in natural ways in many manipulative contexts, such as measuring length or weight with different units, or changing recipes to make more or fewer servings. Ratio also arises when considering the scale of a map, the speed at which one travels, or the price of fruit when one is charged for a number of pieces. Many applications of geometry involve the ratios of sides of similar figures. Most of the challenges in this set can be investigated in more formal language of ratio and proportion, and/or in terms of manipulation of concrete materials.

A Children can use rods to find that two yellow rods are the same length as one orange, and so it will take twice as many yellow rods as an orange rod to make a given length. Similar problems can be phrased with different pairs or rods, for example, dark green and red (where 3 reds make a dark green). More challenging is to use light greens and reds (where 3 red rods are as long as 2 light green rods). See Measurement, Set 24, Challenge B, for a similar challenge using two different sizes of paper clips.

B Children might reason as follows: "It takes 3 cups for 4 servings, and another 4 servings will take 3 more cups. We still need 10 − 8 = 2 servings, which is half of a recipe, which takes 1 1/2 cups. In all we need 3 + 3 + 1 1/2 = 7 1/2 cups of milk." A more direct line of thought might be:

4 servings take 3 cups, and so
2 servings take 1 1/2 cups, and so
5 x 2 servings take 5 x 1 1/2 cups = 7 1/2 cups.

Second graders are not expected to work with fractions symbolically in this way, but if given materials to represent the fractional parts (such as rectangles to represent whole cups, half rectangles to represent the half cups), they can act out this solution.

C This problem (a version of the "cows and chickens" problem described in the Introduction) can be approached by many strategies. Students might simply "guess and check," after noting that one orange costs 20¢ and 2 lemons cost 25¢. They may notice that there must be an even number of lemons. (Why?) They might make a table and notice a pattern, as follows:

Number of oranges	Number of Lemons	Total Price
14	0	$2.80
12	2	$2.65
10	4	$2.50

Since the price is going down by 15¢ each row, the next row (i.e., 8 oranges and 6 lemons) will give the correct price.

D Some students might find this problem easier to think about if they assign a particular value to the weight of the cat. Suppose the cat weighs 300 nickels, then the dog weighs 4 x 300 = 1200 nickels. Since 3 nickels weigh the same as 5 cents, 400 x 3 nickels weigh the same as 400 x 5 cents, and so the dog weighs 2000 cents. The cat's weight in nickels would be worth 300 x 5 cents = $15, while the dog's weight in cents would be worth 2000 cents = $20. Students might try some other possible weights for the cat to convince themselves that the weight of the dog in cents will always be worth more than the weight of the cat in nickels. Older students might reason in terms of a variable, rather than supposing a particular value.

E Students might make their scale drawings at a purely manipulative level using Cuisenaire rods. They can measure with orange rods (10 cm long). For the room, they can measure dimensions with a meter stick or trundle wheel and plan the drawing with orange rods. This technique gives a very concrete meaning to scale, and also familiarizes students with metric units.

F One can assume that the rays of the sun are essentially parallel, and that both the tree and woman are perpendicular to the ground. This problem can be solved by recognizing two similar right triangles, where the base of each is a shadow, and a vertical side is the woman or the tree. For similar triangles, corresponding sides are in proportion. That is, referring to the diagram to the right,

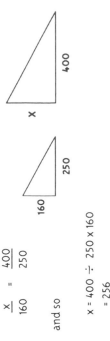

$$\frac{x}{160} = \frac{400}{250}$$

and so

$$x = 400 \div 250 \times 160$$
$$= 256$$

Students might be interested in thinking about how aspects of a "real" situation might change the answer, for example, if the ground slopes in front of the woman but not the tree, or if the shadow is cast by a street lamp and not by the sun. This challenge might precede a challenge to find the height of the school or a flagpole. (See The School Building, Set 32, Challenge E.)

G Perhaps this doesn't make much sense, but it is a classic problem. One might reason that in a given time, if a chicken and a half lays an egg and a half, then in that time the single chicken will lay a single egg. So a chicken lays an egg in a day and a half. It will take these 6 chickens will lay 6 eggs in a day and a half, and 6 chickens will lay 6 eggs in a day and a half. It will take these 6 chickens twice as long as a day and a half to lay a dozen eggs, and so the answer is three days.

H Students will probably approach this problem using a "guess and check" strategy. An elegant and sophisticated solution is to reason that the two cars are approaching each other at a rate of 80 miles per hour. Since they start 100 miles apart, it will take 100 ÷ 80 = 1.25 hours for them to meet. Since Bonnie drives at the rate of 50 miles per hour, she will travel 1.25 x 50 = 62.5 miles before they meet.

CHALLENGE SET : 27

solids

These challenges concern three-dimensional shapes. It might help you to have some models to work with. For some, you can experiment by folding and taping light cardboard to make models. For Challenge G, consider using clay.

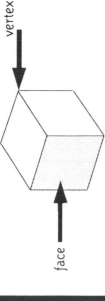

A. Find the Block

Find a block in the classroom which has faces like these.

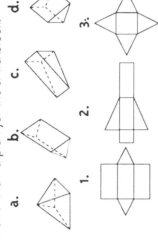

Find another block, and draw its faces.

B. Which One Doesn't Belong?

a.

b.

c.

d.

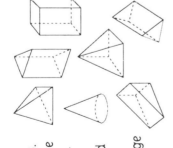

Explain why.

Can you find more than one possible answer?

C. Match the Plans

Match the blocks to the plans which will make them. Draw a plan for the extra block.

a.   b.   c.   d.

1.   2.   3.

D. A Square Peg in a Round Hole?

Describe a solid that can be put through both of these holes so that the solid touches the edges all around.

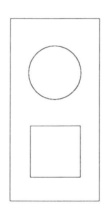

E. Guess My Solid

It has four triangular faces.
It has five square faces.
It has only nine faces.

Can you draw a plan for it?

F. What Could It Be?

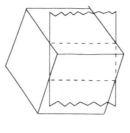

vertex

face

A cube has 6 faces and 8 vertices.

A mystery solid has 8 faces and 12 vertices.

What could it be?

G. Slicing a Cube

If a plane cuts a cube as shown, the cut forms a rectangle.

What other shapes can you get when a plane cuts a cube?

(Try this for other shapes, such as a cylinder, a cone, or a sphere.)

H. Ribbon on a Box

Here are three ways of putting ribbon on a box which measures 10 cm x 20 cm x 5 cm.

Which takes the most ribbon? the least?

a.   b.   c.

These challenges are about the geometry of solids. Spatial visualization skills developed through this study are important in many areas of life — for example, when trying to assemble a toy or a piece of furniture from a visual plan, as well as in mathematics. The study of solids may allow use of unexpected strengths of students who do not excel in more numerical areas of mathematics.

Students whose school experience of three-dimensional geometry is restricted to a two-dimensional page often have difficulty in this area. It is important for students to have many opportunities to construct and handle models of solids. Teachers can buy specially made construction kits and sets of solids, or can find inexpensive alternatives, many of which can involve students creatively while developing their spatial skills. Sometimes interesting models of solids can be found as everyday objects or packaging materials or in early childhood classrooms, in the block corner. Also some commonly available materials such as milk cartons or cereal boxes can be cut, folded and taped to make models of more unusual solids. Once students have seen a few models, they might be able to "see" new solids in a milk carton.

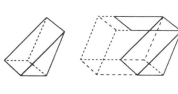

triangular prism   square pyramid   12-faced polyhedron

Once advantage of these easily made and "free" materials is that they can also be cut apart to show plans for solids. Photographs of buildings, toys, furniture, packages, etc. also may provide more "real" images of solids than abstract line drawings.

There are additional challenges related to solids in Cubes, Set 6; Attribute Sets, Set 7, Challenge F; Probability, Set 28, Challenge E; and Halloween, Set 30, Challenge E.

The Mathematical Toolbox   © 1992 Cuisenaire Company of America, Inc.

A This solid is known to kindergarten children as a "ramp" in the block corner, and to older students as "a triangular prism." One can easily be made by cutting a cereal box as shown. This problem might be accompanied by a display of several solids. Children can be encouraged to make similar puzzles for other blocks in the class collection.

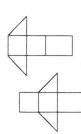

B This challenge shows how the format of Which One is Different?, Set 14, can be applied to solids. There are at least two answers to this question: (a) is the only one which is not a "polyhedron" (made up of flat sides), while (b) is the only one which is not a "pyramid," a solid with a flat base the edges of which are all connected to a point. If possible, present this problem with several models of solids, rather than just diagrams.

C Solid (a) goes with plan (3), (b) goes with (1), and (c) goes with (2). Solid (d) goes with any of the plans shown to the right, although other plans are possible. If possible, display this problem with actual solids, and cut-out plans so that students can try folding up the plans to check their answers.

D A "short" cylinder will satisfy this condition. This problem can be phrased in terms of shadows, that is, "What shape can cast these shadows?" If you have an overhead projector available, you can have students experiment with what shadows a solid will make. A classic and more difficult problem is to find a solid that will just fit in the three holes shown. One way to investigate this is with clay. Try first making a cylinder which will fit exactly through the circular and square holes, then cut it with a

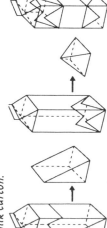

knife or wire to make a solid which will also fit exactly through the other hole.

E Let students experiment with taping the cut-out pieces. If students really need an additional hint, you might add "It looks like a cube glued to a pyramid." One possible plan is shown. As a follow-up, have a child select a secret solid and give only verbal clues to classmates.

F One answer to this question is a hexagonal prism. Another way to give clues is more sensory. Put a solid in a closed box and see if children can figure out what it is from moving the box around. They should be able to feel and/or hear if it rolls or slides, or how far it must be tipped before it falls over, etc. If children examine many solids and make a chart of the number of edges (E), faces (F) and vertices (V), they can be challenged to find a pattern. (The fact that V − E + F = 2 for any solid without holes, is known as Euler's Formula.)

G You can get many shapes in this way — squares, rectangles, trapezoids, various triangles, even a hexagon. If you or your students have difficult visualizing these cuts, try using a block of clay or colored water in a transparent plastic cube.

H In order, from most to least, the lengths of ribbon required are (c). (a). (b). This assumes that the same amount of ribbon is used for each bow. Method (a) takes 2 x 10 + 2 x 20 + 4 x 5 = 80 cm of ribbon, not counting the bow. The lengths for (b) and (c) will depend on how far apart are the parallel ribbon pieces on the top of the box. You can find these lengths using the Pythagorean Theorem. You can present this problem on an actual box.

CHALLENGE SET : 28

probability

We deal with probability whenever we encounter events that are not certain — what we will roll on a die in a game, what the weather will be tomorrow, what kind of nut we'll get if we reach into a bowl of mixed nuts without looking. The challenges in this set involve some ways of thinking about probability.

A. What Is in the Bag?

There are 4 chips in this bag. Reach in, *without looking*, and select a chip. Look at it, and keep a record. Then replace it and try again. Do it 10 times in all.

Then write your prediction for what chips are in the bag.

B. Different Dice

Opposite faces of these dice have the same value.

Suppose that you can pick one of these dice, roll it, and get the number of dollars shown on top. Which die would you choose? Why?

C. A Spinner

If you spin this spinner 50 times, how many times do you expect it to land on the black area?

D. A Probability Line

Can you think of events that belong at the points marked on the "probability line?" (An event that can never happen has probability 0, and one that must happen has probability 1.)

E. Design a Die

Design a solid that could be used as a die to pick the numbers 1, 2, 3, 4.

Each number should have the same probability of being picked.

F. Attendance

How many absences will there be in our class next week?

What information do you need to make a good prediction?

G. Marbles

How could you put marbles in a bag so that the probability of picking a red marble is $1/2$, a green marble is $1/4$, and a black marble is $1/8$?

H. Siblings

Suppose that a generous millionaire will select three children at random from our class, and take them out to a movie with all of their siblings.

What is the probability that exactly four children will go to the movie?

Commentary: 28
PROBABILTY

This set of challenges concerns probability. The investigation of probability provides an opportunity for students of all ages to discover connections with other areas of mathematics (graphing measurement, solid geometry, ratio are illustrated below) and many aspects of their lives. The NCTM Curriculum and Evaluation Standards for School Mathematics states: "The study of probability in grades 5–8 should not focus on developing formulas or computing the likelihood of events pictured in texts. Students should actively explore situations by experimenting and simulating probability models." This is even more true for younger children. Initial work should build intuition through many physical experiments. Building of mathematical models for probability should be done only after such intuition is well established.

A You will need to set this up first by putting chips in the bag, perhaps 3 reds and 1 blue, or 2 reds, 1 white, 1 blue. (You can use other small objects than chips. However, be sure children cannot tell them apart just by feeling them.) This challenge will encourage students to find some way to keep records of the chips they select. When discussing students' results, be sure to compare how they did this — possibly with a list, or with tally marks, or maybe with a graph. You can encourage several students to combine their findings, possibly coloring in squares on grid paper to show their totals in a bar graph form. Underlying this problem is the idea of ratio, that if you pick a red chip about twice as often as a blue chip, there are probably twice as many reds as blues in the bag. Encourage students to use informal language of probability to discuss when they are *certain* that they know what color chips are in the bag versus when they just *think* they know.

B Students should have the dice available to experiment with. You might be able to find suitable ready-made boxes or small blocks, or you could make such dice by gluing small cubes together. This activi-

ty should lead to discussion of how all faces are equally likely to land up for a die which is a true cube, but for the second die, a long rectangular face is more likely (hence a winning of \$2 or \$3), and for the third die, a square face is more likely (hence a winning of \$1). To vary the problem, you can put different numbers on the faces. Don't worry about building a formal mathematical model for this situation at this point. Students might verify their answers by rolling each die a large number of times and graphing their results.

C Many students will say that the arrow is more likely to point to the white area than any other. They are considering measurement of area of the regions, rather than measurement of *angle*. When building models for probability, it is important to be sure what aspects of the situation are relevant. To convince students that angle is the aspect of the spinner that they should consider, make this device: Cut a circular hole in the front of a folder, and attach a spinner to the inside so that it shows through the hole, but is off-center. Then on the inside of the folder draw a large spinner pattern centered on the spinner's hole. Ask students the "problem" with the cover closed. Then open the cover and ask the question again. How would the spinner "know" whether the cover was closed or not?

front cover

back cover

D This problem leads to lively discussion. For example, can one be *sure* that a coin won't land on its side? What *can* one really be sure about? You might want to phrase the question in terms of particular probability devices, for example, a deck of cards, dice, or spinners.

E It is not difficult to design a solid that selects numbers 1–4 (for example, change the 5 and 6 on a standard die to be 1 and 2), but it is more diffi-

cult to ensure that each number is equally likely to be picked. Students might suggest a long square prism, for example, an orange Cuisenaire rod, on the assumption that it will never land on a square end, but presumably this *could* happen. One solution is a tetrahedron, but as a die this has the disadvantage that you can't read the number that is face down. If you double or triple the number of faces to get 8 (labeling them 1, 1, 2, 2, 3, 3, 4, 4) or a dodecahedron (12 faces), you might think of using an octahedron (8 faces) or a dodecahedron (12 faces). (Both are available commercially as polyhedral dice.) A curriculum unit based on this idea, "Dice Design", was developed by the Unified Science and Mathematics in Elementary School (USMES). The description of teachers' logs of students' thinking is interesting.

F To approach this challenge, students will need to collect data about absences in the recent past. It might also be interesting to try to get data from previous years. Are there any seasonal events that would effect the number of absences? This challenge might motivate a study of how often the weather report is correct.

G There are many solutions to this problem. The simplest uses 8 marbles, with 1 black, 2 green and 4 red, and 1 of some other color. The problem becomes more difficult if you change the fractions.

H To answer this problem, students must first collect data on the number of siblings of each student. The only way that exactly four students will go to the movie is if two of the students selected have no siblings and one has exactly one. Students might list the groups of students matching this description, or they might approach it through more abstract combinatorial reasoning.

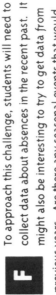

square prism

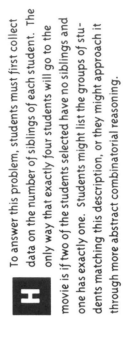

tetrahedron

dodecahedron

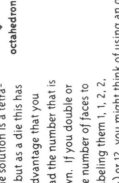

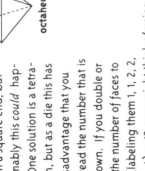

octahedron

CHALLENGE SET : 29

measurement of time

Time goes by all the time and we are often not even aware of it. The challenges in this set are about ways to measure time. For Challenge A you need two different sand timers, such as those sometimes used in games or to time eggs cooking. For Challenge B you need a clock with a second hand. A calculator is recommended for the later challenges.

A. Sand Timers

Use two different sand timers.

Which timer will take longer for the sand to run through?

Start the timers at the same time. Turn the quicker one over as soon as it runs out.

How many times will the quicker one run out before the slower one runs out?

B. Estimate How Many

How many times can you stand up and sit down in a minute?

How many times can you draw ⊠ in a minute?

Think of another thing to do as many times as possible in a minute. Estimate what you can do, then try it.

C. Birthdays and New Year's Eves

a. How many New Year's Eves have you been alive? How many birthdays have you had? Are the numbers always the same?

b. I've been alive for 18 New Year's Eves, but I've only had 4 birthdays. When was I born?

D. Matching Hands

The two hands of a clock overlap exactly at 12 o'clock, but also at other times. How often during the day does this happen?

Which is correct more of the time, a clock that doesn't work at all, or a clock that loses 1 minute each hour?

E. Special Times

We celebrate the end of the year and the start of a new one— but why not find other special times to celebrate? For example, when is the millionth second of this year? The millionth minute?

F. Ancient Queens

Boadicea died 129 years after Cleopatra was born. Their combined ages were 100 years. Cleopatra died in 30 B.C.

When was Boadicea born?

G. De Morgan's Birth

Augustus De Morgan, the mathematician, who died in 1871, boasted that he was x years old in the year x^2. Can you give the year in which De Morgan was born?

Can anyone now living make this claim?

H. How Old?

In 1930 a man reported that the age of his uncle when he died was one twenty-ninth of the year of his uncle's birth. How old was his uncle in 1900?

Commentary: 29
MEASUREMENT OF TIME

These challenges concern the passage and measurement of time. (Calendars, Set 34, is related in that it explores the ways in which we break time into months and weeks, and how numbers are written in an array to express this.)

Measurement of time is learned in a sequence of stages, similar to that for learning about measurement in general. (See the commentary on Measurement, Set 24.) In school, learning about time is often confused with learning to read a clock. "Time" won't fit on a printed page. Sometimes children are taught a few isolated positions of clock hands before they have any sense of what is being measured, or how long a minute is. Children learn best what is meaningful to them. The study of time measurement should be incorporated into the day. If you want children to learn about how a clock works, use a class clock, and draw how the clock will look when something special is to happen. That will encourage children to look at the clock over time and to see how it changes.

A
Results will depend on your materials. Sand clocks can be made from clear plastic cups taped together, filled with salt. You can melt a small hole in the bottom of the cups with a heated skewer or knitting needle. For a small sand clock, you might use one that comes with a commercial game.

B
Results of these questions are often surprising. A minute can seem like an awfully long time, or an awfully short time, depending on what one is doing. You might ask children if they think they can hold their breath for a minute. It is a challenge! Seeing how many times you can stand up and sit down in a minute will

be a noisy activity, but will let off a lot of pent-up energy. Drawing the square with an "X" in the middle may produce some interesting strategies. One first-grade child who drew a very large number of these squares in a minute did it by looking ahead to how the squares fit together — he did it with the steps shown.

C
Children with birthdays this year before the question in part a is posed will have different answers from children whose birthdays are ahead. The answer to the question in part b is February 29, in a leap year. Children might be amused by the somewhat silly plot of Gilbert and Sullivan's operetta, *The Pirates of Penzance*, which hinges on the fact that young Frederick, through the stupidity and poor hearing of his nursemaid, is apprenticed to a *pilot* as his parents intended) until his twenty-first birthday. His birthday, it develops, was on February 29 in a leap year, and so when he has lived 21 years, he has in fact had only 5 birthdays. A song explains this, "A paradox, a paradox, a most ingenious paradox."

D
The hands will overlap 22 times. It may be tricky to find the exact times. It's 1:05, 2:10, 3:15, ... a little after the times 1:05, 2:10, 3:15, ... 9:45,10:50 — then one is back to 12:00.

Students in later grades can be asked many interesting questions about the angle between the two hands. For example how often are the two hands at right angles? Children should be asked to explain why the hand positions drawn to the right actually never occur. Where should the hour hand be at 3:30?

E
A calculator is suggested here. Since there are over 600,000 seconds in a week, the millionth second of 1990 occurred in the second week of

the year. There are 60 x 60 x 24 = 86,400 seconds in a day. In 11 days, there are 11 x 86,400 = 950,400 seconds, which is 49,600 short of one million. The millionth second is on January 12, at 13 hours, 46 minutes and 40 seconds into the day, that is, a little after 1:46 PM. If you happen to meet a math class at this time, consider a celebration. Maybe the great event could be announced on the loudspeaker.

What else can you find to celebrate? There are only about half a million minutes in a year. Also see Estimation, Set 20, Challenge E, and the suggestion there for using the book, *How Much Is a Million?*

F
There were 29 (or 129 − 100) years between Cleopatra's death and Boadicea's birth, so the answer is 1 B.C., 29 years after 30 B.C. Students might find this easier to visualize if they draw a number line to represent the lifespans. This challenge and the next two are from *536 Puzzles and Curious Problems* by Henry Ernest Dudeney (Scribner's, 1967).

G
If you try finding possible values for x^2, you will find that $42^2 = 1764$, $43^2 = 1849$ and $44^2 = 1936$. The only possible date is 1849, because De Morgan died in 1871, and so he must have been 43 in 1849. Notice that a person who was 44 in 1980 could also make this claim.

H
The year of the uncle's birth was a multiple of 29. $29 \times 63 = 1827$ is ruled out because the question implies that the uncle was alive in 1900. $29 \times 65 = 1885$ is ruled out because the uncle would not have been dead by 1930. However, $29 \times 64 = 1856$ would mean he died in 1920 at age 64. So he was born in 1856 and was 44 in 1900.

A Final Note About Time...

"When is there time to expose children to all of the exciting mathematics I'd like to?" teachers often ask. There is no easy answer. Perhaps some of the challenges in this book allow you to tuck interesting ideas into small pockets of time. As they say about child-rearing, "quality time" is what one should aim for!

CHALLENGE SET : 30

halloween

In late October, signs of Halloween are everywhere. Stores present huge displays of candy, children (and adults, too!) plan costumes, and pictures of bats, black cats, witches, jack-o'-lanterns abound. All of this activity can be looked at with a mathematical eye. These challenges show some of the possibilities.

F. The Great(er) Pumpkin

You need two pumpkins of different sizes. How much "bigger" is the bigger pumpkin than the smaller?

Estimate:

• how many times more seeds it has;

• how many times more volume it has;

• how many times heavier it is.

G. Candy Corn

Count out 100 brown candy corn and mix them into a bag of regular candy corn. Put the mixture in a jar.

I put 100 brown candy corn in the jar. How many candy corn are there in all?

H. Witch's Brew

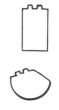

A witch is making a brew requiring 4 cups of bat's blood.

She only has two measures, which hold 7 cups and 10 cups.

How can she use her measures to measure exactly 4 cups?

C. Pirates

On Halloween 18 pirates came to my door for trick-or-treat. 11 had eye patches. 9 had cutlasses. 3 had neither cutlasses nor eye patches.

How many pirates had *both* cutlasses *and* eye patches?

D. Bats and Cats

As I entered a haunted house, some bats and some cats rushed out. I was scared, but I managed to count 50 eyes. I also counted 78 legs.

How many cats rushed out?

E. Costume Hats

Some children made cardboard hats for their Halloween costumes. Which pattern goes with each hat? What sort of a hat would the leftover pattern make?

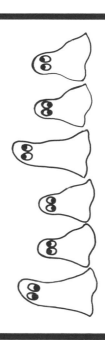

A. Jack-o'-lanterns

Which one is different? Why?

Can you find more than one answer?

B. Whooo's Next?

What comes next? Why?

Can you see two patterns at once?

The Mathematical Toolbox   © 1992 Cuisenaire Company of America, Inc.

These challenges are all about Halloween. Relating mathematics to such an exciting event may foster appreciation of "Mathematical Connections" — one of the thirteen curriculum standards for school mathematics for grades K-8 recommended by the National Council of Teachers of Mathematics (1989). In these challenges, many different mathematical topics are tied into images or activities surrounding Halloween — classification, patterns, non-routine problem-solving, construction of solids, counting, estimation, and measurement of weight and volume.

Some challenges may be familiar to you from other contexts. This collection is an example of how problems can be adapted to build on current enthusiasms of a class. If Halloween is not an appropriate context for your class, try stating these problems in terms related to another holiday or celebration (Thanksgiving? birthday parties?) or a class interest (dinosaurs? a trip to the zoo?).

A This challenge has two answers. Encourage students to find and describe both. (They should look at the eyes, or the stems.) An extension of this challenge is to ask students to design a similar one that has three, or even four, valid answers. (See Which One Is Different?, Set 14, for more challenges in this format.) The jack-o'-lanterns suggest creation of an attribute set (see Attribute Sets, Set 7) with these attributes: stem (pointing right or left): eyes (pointing up or down); and number of teeth (1, 2 or 3). If more attributes are desired, you can change the shape of the nose, or the expression of the mouth.

B This pattern can be seen in two different ways. You might see the pattern of eyes (looking down, up, down, up, ...) superimposed on the pattern of size (big, small, small, big, small, small, ...). On the other hand, if more pieces are added, one might simply see a repeating pattern of six elements.

C There are many ways to think about this problem. One purely numerical approach is to realize that since 11 of the 18 pirates had eye patches, 7 of them did not have patches. Of these 7, 3 did not have cutlasses, and so 4 had cutlasses and no eye patches. Since 9 had cutlasses, 9 − 4 had cutlasses and eye patches. Compare this way of reasoning with the use of a visual representation as shown to the right (often called a "Venn diagram"). The same sequence of steps as before can lead to filling in numbers to show how many pirates belong in each region.

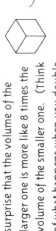

Eyepatches Cutlasses

6   5   4

11   9   3

18 Pirates

D This is an example of the "cows and chickens" problem which is discussed in the Introduction. Students will first have to agree that bats have two legs. This problem usually inspires many different approaches. One is a guess and check strategy. Students might guess, say, 10 cats, accounting for 20 of the eyes, and so there would be 30 eyes coming from bats, or 15 bats. That would mean there are 10 × 4 = 40 cat legs, and 15 × 2 = 30 bat legs, making 70 legs in all. This is too few legs, and so a second guess might be more cats, say 12 (giving 48 cat legs and 26 bat legs, or 74 in all). Students might then see the pattern that adding one cat adds two more legs, and so at this point might reason that there must be 12 ÷ 2 = 14 cats. Another strategy is to try the extreme case: if the 25 animals were all bats, there would be 50 legs, which is 28 legs too few, and so there must be 28 ÷ 2 = 14 cats, since each cat replacing a bat adds 2 more legs.

E Students can experiment with cut-out pieces of paper to verify which patterns match which hats. They could also cut apart common cardboard materials similar to these hats — paper cups or cardboard tubes. A challenging extension of this problem is to figure out how much of the circle should be cut out to make a conical hat which is as tall as it is wide at the base.

F This problem raises many issues about measurement. For example, how can one measure volume of a pumpkin? Students might suggest chopping it up and measuring with cups. Much easier (although possibly a bit messy) is to measure by "displacement." Submerge the pumpkin in a bucket of water and measure the water displaced. For a large pumpkin, you may have difficulty in finding a large enough bucket. You can also use a rectangular sink. If the entire pumpkin cannot be submerged, marked a line approximately around the middle, measure water displaced by submerging just the lower part, then turn it over and repeat with the other part.

Many students will estimate that a pumpkin with twice the diameter of another will have twice the volume, and also twice the weight. It may come as a surprise that the volume of the larger one is more like 8 times the volume of the smaller one. (Think of what happens when you double the dimensions of a cube. It takes 8 of the original cubes to build it. The same relationship applies to any shape.) An interesting question is whether larger pumpkins have more seeds than smaller ones. Perhaps several classes could collect data related to this.

G This question encourages students to estimate a ratio (brown to orange candy corn) and then use it to make their estimate of the total number. You might allow students to take out a scoopful of the mixed candy corn and check the ratio in their sample. This is actually a model of a method used in estimating natural populations which cannot be counted directly, such as fish in a lake. A specific number of marked fish are released, and then the ratio of marked to unmarked fish which are caught is noted. This sampling technique is well-presented for students in the videotape *The Challenge of the Unknown*.

H One solution is to fill the 7-cup measure, pour it into the 10-cup measure (leaving a space of 3 cups), then refill the 7-cup and pour enough into the 10-cup measure to fill it, leaving just 4 cups in the 7-cup measure. (This requires a good supply of bat's blood!)

CHALLENGE SET : 31

patchwork quilts

These challenges are about patchwork patterns used in quilts. While some patchwork quilts are "crazy," using random shapes, most are carefully planned and are based on geometric relationships. When you make one of these geometric quilts from many small pieces of different fabrics, you must be very exact in your measurements.

F. Angles

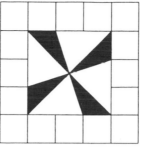

What are the angle measures of the diamond from which this pattern is made?

G. Percent

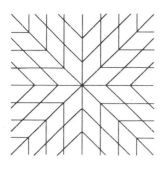

What percent of the area of this pattern is black?

H. Length

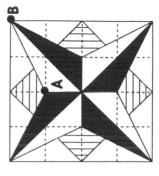

What is the length of line segment AB if the side of the whole square measures 40 cm?

C. Area

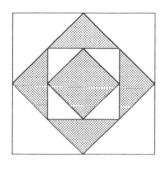

What is the area of each piece if the whole square measures 20 cm on each side?

D. Symmetry

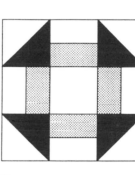

Color this pattern in different ways, so that it has:
- exactly 1 line of symmetry
- exactly 2 lines of symmetry
- exactly 4 lines of symmetry
- rotational but not line symmetry.

E. Fractions

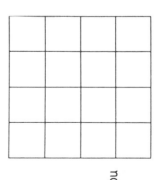

What fraction of the whole square is the square piece? the triangular piece? the rectangular piece?

A. Squares and Triangles

How many squares do you see?

How many triangles do you see?

B. Making Patterns

Fill in each square in the grid with a pattern like this:

Use three colors.

You can turn the pattern any way you want.

The Mathematical Toolbox

Traditional patchwork patterns provide a wonderful springboard for mathematics. They are part of our cultural heritage, they are visually appealing, and students can be involved creatively in their design. These challenges suggest a few ways in which mathematics can arise through the study of patchwork patterns.

Patchwork patterns can provide a motivation for students to write their own challenges. When students have been exposed to several of the geometric ideas which arise in these challenges, show them a new patchwork pattern, and ask them to write a mathematical question about it.

Another approach is to have each of them design a pattern based on the same size of square. Select 4 to 6 of them and use the Which One Is Different? format. (See Challenge Set 14 on this.) Or students might write a few clues for their pattern, possibly involving some of the mathematical topics touched on in this book of challenges. One student's set of clues can be displayed with a number of the patterns, and other students can be asked to figure out which pattern (or patterns) the clues apply to. Discuss how to write the fewest possible clues so that just one pattern is indicated.

Students might be able to use their patterns to make a fabric quilt or wall hanging to hang in the school or to be raffled as a fund-raiser.

Two excellent sources for patterns are The Perfect Patchwork Primer by Beth Gutcheon (Penguin, 1973) and Patchwork Patterns by Jinny Beyer (EPM Publications, Inc., 1979).

A Children may initially see only the small squares and triangles. Encourage them to see that there are squares and triangles of several different sizes.
Younger children may not make an exhaustive search. To count all squares and triangles in the pattern, one needs to have a systematic counting strategy. For example, when counting squares, notice that there are 13 of the smallest ones, 4 2-by-2 squares (made up of 4 small ones), 1 3-by-3,

and of course, the large boundary square. Similarly, they can find triangles as drawn below.

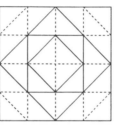

B This challenge does not have a "correct" solution. The aim is to create an attractive pattern. You might introduce the challenge by having students fold a square piece of paper to make the 16 squares. With a ruler they can draw in diagonals, and then color the pattern shown in each square, using any three colors they wish. If they then cut up their squares, they can explore ways to rearrange the pieces. At the end of the week, look at the varied solutions and discuss how they are alike and different.

C Students might divide the whole square into 16 small squares, and see that every piece is made up of some number of triangles, each of which is half of a small square, the size of the smallest white triangle in the pattern. Since the area of the whole square is 400 square centimeters, the area of this smallest triangle is 400 ÷ 32 = 12.5 cm². They might also think in terms of paper folding, seeing what happens as corners are folded in.

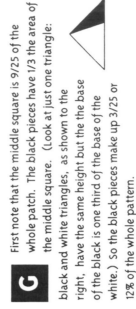

D Here are some solutions:

1 line of symmetry   2 lines of symmetry

4 lines of symmetry   rotational, but not line symmetry

You can extend this challenge: Can you color to have 0 lines of symmetry? (Yes.) 3 lines of symmetry? (No.) line symmetry but not rotational symmetry? (Yes. See the first example above.)

E To give students a hint, you might tell them that this pattern is called a "nine-patch." (Can they see why?) The white square in the center is 1/9 of the whole patch, and since the triangle and rectangle are each 1/2 of the square piece, each is 1/18 of the whole patch. You can extend this problem by asking — What fraction of the patch is black? (4/18 or 2/9) white? (10/18 or 5/9) striped? (4/18 or 2/9)

F Students might reason that eight congruent angles fit together at the center to make 360° (or some might see that two make 90°) and so the smaller angle must measure 45°. The larger angle together with the smaller makes a straight angle or 180°, and so measures 135°. Students can verify that the angle sum of the diamond is 360°. Students can compare this "starburst" pattern with a similar one made with rhombuses with the smaller angle of 60°.

G First note that the middle square is 9/25 of the whole patch. The black pieces have 1/3 the area of the middle square. (Look at just one triangle, black and white triangles, as shown to the right, have the same height but the the base of the black is one third of the base of the white.) So the black pieces make up 3/25 or 12% of the whole pattern.

H Students should see that this line segment is the hypotenuse h of a triangle with other sides 20 and 10 cm. Thus:

$$h^2 = 20^2 + 10^2$$
$$h = \sqrt{400 + 100} = \sqrt{500}$$
$$h = \sqrt{100 \times 5} = 10\sqrt{5}$$

20 cm   10 cm $h = \sqrt{500}$

CHALLENGE SET : 32

the school building

There are many mathematical questions that you can ask about a school building. The ones on this page relate to counting, estimation, measurement of length, perimeter, area, volume, and electricity, and geometric patterns.

Think of others that are especially relevant to your own building.

F. Electricity

How many kilowatts are used by our school building in a full week?

G. Comparing Rooms

Select two different classrooms.

Which has more floor space? wall space? window space? air?

H. Radio Signals

Suppose that the range of a radio signal is 10 meters. How many people could receive a signal sent out from the door of our classroom at 9:00 A.M. on a Friday morning?

C. Tilings

How many different tiling patterns are there in our school?

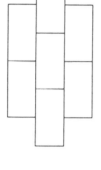

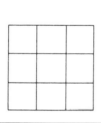

D. A New Coat of Paint

Suppose we want to paint our classroom. How much paint will it take?

E. How High?

How high is the tallest part of our school building?

How could we find out?

A. Doors

How many doors are on this floor of our school building?

B. String

How many meters of string would it take to stretch all around the base of our building, at ground level?

Commentary: 32
THE SCHOOL BUILDING

These challenges indicate how our built environment can provide a context for mathematical investigations. Some challenges require students to do further research. Students should be encouraged to examine their surroundings with a mathematical eye. They could be challenged to think of a new mathematical question about their school building.

A Children might initially just count classrooms, thinking that each classroom has a door. But if encouraged to look more closely, they will probably find that each class also has doors on closets, and also on items, such as pet cages, doll houses, toy cars, etc. To provide a hint, you might find such a non-standard door in the classroom and tell children to look, for example, for a door which is as tall as an orange Cuisenaire rod.

B When posing this problem to older children, you might use the word "perimeter." Stating the question in informal language illustrates how children can often experience mathematical concepts in an intuitive way before they are formalized later in their school experience. If children draw a rough floor plan of their school, they will probably realize that the measuring can be simplified because certain lengths will be the same — for example, two opposite sides of a rectangle.

C Even if your school building uses only square or rectangular tiles, you may find that they are arranged in different tiling patterns. Another common tiling pattern is the hexagonal one shown below.

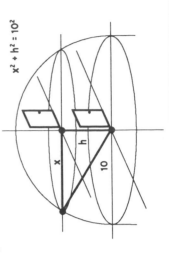

If students expand their search to the school neighborhood or to photographs, they will find many others.

D This question requires more information. Try to have students ask for the missing data before you mention it. A paint can will provide an estimate of the area it will cover. Will the room require one or two coats? Do you plan to paint the ceiling? Students will need to find the area of wall to be painted. They may do this by breaking the wall up into rectangles. They may simplify the measurement process by realizing that certain wall measures are the same. Another approach might be to find the area of the total wall space assuming there are no doors or windows, and then to subtract parts that won't be painted.

E This challenge can be approached by many strategies. First, students might decide what is meant by "how high?" Is it above the ground level (and if so, is the ground on which the school is built flat?) or height above sea level? The building itself might offer ways to estimate the height. Perhaps there are bricks that can be measured directly, and then counted. Perhaps one floor can be measured with string dropped from a window, and then this measure multiplied by the number of floors. Another method is to compare an object whose height is known (say, a person) with the height of the building, using a thumb held at arm's length as a sort of ruler.

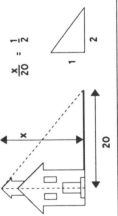

If the building casts a shadow on level ground, students might measure the length of the shadow of the building, and also the length of the shadow of a meter stick.

$$\frac{x}{20} = \frac{1}{2}$$

F The answer to this question can be found with the cooperation of the school custodian, who might allow a class visit to the school's electricity meter.

To estimate, students might examine wattage of light bulbs, and estimate how long they are turned on each week. The challenge might motivate investigation of how students can save money on their family's electricity bills by turning off unneeded lights.

G Students should examine both rooms and estimate answers, before actually measuring. They should be encouraged to use the terms "area" and "volume." As an extension, ask them to improve the design of their classroom. Should it have more or less wall space, window space, floor space, volume? What are the constraints that an architect might have to work with when designing a classroom?

H Students may initially think only of people on their floor of the building when approaching this question. But what about people in the classroom directly overhead or underneath? They should realize that they need to find out how many people are within a sphere of radius 10 meters and centered at the door of the classroom. They may need to apply the Pythagorean Theorem to find the size of the circle on the floor above them within which the radio signal could be heard. That is, they should find out how high above them the next floor is (h in the diagram below) and then find the radius x of the circle with center directly over the "radio transmitter" which represents the points furthest away at which the signal could be heard.

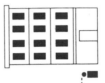

$$x^2 + h^2 = 10^2$$

CHALLENGE SET : 33

april fool's day

There are many tricks and jokes about mathematics. Do you "get" these ones?

Perhaps you can add to this collection.

A. Birds on a Wire

Five birds were sitting on a telephone wire. A farmer shot two of them.

How many were left sitting on the wire?

B. Do You Trust Your Eyes?

Which is longer, line segment AB or line segment CD?

C. Boiling Eggs

If it takes five minutes to boil one egg, how long does it take to boil three eggs?

D. Triangles

How many triangles are in this diagram?

E. St. Ives

As I was going to St. Ives, I met a man with seven wives.

Every wife had seven sacks, every sack had seven cats,

Every cat had seven kits. Kits. cats, sacks wives,

How many were going to St. Ives?

F. What Is It?

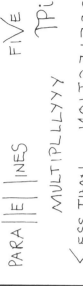

√COFFIN

G. Riddles

What do they call those who are opposed to metrication?

Why did they put the mathematician in prison?

Why is the meter stick such a stubborn ruler?

H. MatheMADics

These mathematical words contain visual tricks. Do you "get" them?

PARA||E||||NES   FIVE

MULTIPLLLYYY   TTPi

<ESS THAN   NOITCELFER

FACTOR.IAL

Make up some more of your own.

In honor of April Fool's Day, here are some challenges which might be called mathematical jokes. The intent is to inject a "light touch" into the teaching of mathematics. Some of these are just for fun, but others might get across the message that one has to read carefully.

It is important to communicate that mathematics can entertain and amuse. There are extensive sources of "recreational mathematics" in popular literature — for example, in children's corners of many newspapers. Some popular cartoon strips occasionally refer to mathematics. Children should realize that while mathematics has a serious role in many aspects of our lives, it is also a plaything. Many children and adults find mathematical puzzles valuable for their own sake. You might ask students to collect and bring in mathematical jokes or entertainments. You can use them to reduce anxiety and tension on a test, or simply to motivate and amuse. Challenges in some other sets resemble some common "recreational" puzzles, such as those in Toothpicks, Set 9, or Tangrams, Set 4.

Older students might be entertained by a classic joke, comparing how a physicist, a mathematician and an engineer all come to the conclusion that all odd numbers greater than one are prime. To understand the joke, they must have heard of "proof by induction" where one shows that something is true for every number in a set by first showing that it is true for the lowest number in a set, and then showing that if it is true for one number, it is true for the next one. The physicist says "3 is prime, 5 is prime, 7 is prime, 9 is not prime — that's experimental error — 11 is prime, 13 is prime, so all odd numbers are prime." The mathematician says "3 is prime, 5 is prime, 7 is prime, it is true by induction." Finally the engineer says "3 is prime, 5 is prime, 7 is prime, 9 is prime, 11 is prime, all odd numbers are prime."

In the same general mood, consider use of light-hearted music related to mathematics. Here are three examples. Perhaps you know of others.

Tom Lehrer's song "New Math" is about doing subtraction in base eight. The tune itself is catchy, and some of the humor is typical of Lehrer's dark side, but students can actually follow the steps in this algorithm.

The somewhat silly plot of the operetta, The Pirates of Penzance by Gilbert and Sullivan, is described in Measurement of Time, Set 29. A song explains this as, "A paradox, a paradox, a most ingenious paradox."

For a mathematician, how pleasing to have the chorus of an amusing song contain the phrase "Quid Erat Demonstrandum" or "Q.E.D." In Leonard Bernstein's comic opera Candide, the learned Pangloss uses example after example to prove that all is for the best in "The Best of All Possible Worlds."

A No birds will be left. Those which were not shot would have flown away at the sound of the gun.

B If you draw this, measure the horizontal segments carefully. They should be exactly the same, although the added diagonals make the one on the left look longer. Consideration of optical illusions can lead children to think about when they can trust their eyes and when they cannot. There are many good sources for optical illusions. *The Optical Illusion Book* by Seymour Simon (William Morrow and Company, New York, 1984) gives many examples, and also discusses why we are fooled. Some other optical illusion which are easy to draw are these:

Which line segment is longer, AB or CD?

Which is on the continuation of the line from E — F or G? (Is your answer the same if you turn the page so that the line from E is horizontal?)

(AB and CD should be exactly the same length, and F should be on be the continuation of the line from E.)

C Five minutes (unless you are concerned about the very slight effect of a cool egg on the simmering water). You might consider throwing problems like this one in with standard multiplication word problems, and help students to articulate what multiplication really means.

D There are no triangles in the diagram, since triangles must have straight sides. (But of course most sensible people will ask for a "triangle" in a pizza shop.) This diagram shows a nice construction that children can do, either with a compass, or just by tracing around a circle. They might fill in line segments between all the intersection points, and form a grid from equilateral triangles. Then ask this question again. The diagram shown to the right contains 38 triangles. Students might approach this problem by counting the various sizes, as shown below.

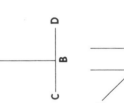

12	6	2
12	6	6
12	12	2

E Just one... myself. This is a very old joke. A version of it appears in the Rhind papyrus from Egypt.

F Root bier, wrecked angle, Noah's Arc, signed numbers, hy pot en use. Ask your students to design further visual riddles using mathematical vocabulary. This and the next two come from *Mathematics and Humor*, ed. Azzolino, Silvey & Hughes, NCTM.

G De feet ists. He tried to kil o meter. Because it won't give an inch. (Ouch!)

H Pages 30-31 of the above-mentioned book contain many more examples. You might have students look up a list of vocabulary words they have been using, and try to interpret them like these 'matheMADics.'

CHALLENGE SET : 34

calendars

A calendar shows how each day is assigned to a month, a date, and a weekday. Most calendars present the numbers in a particular way, in an array. There are a lot of mathematical questions you can ask about a calendar. Some can be done using any month's calendar, while others are more specific. These challenges were written in 1990. Adapt them for the current year.

F. The Passing of 1990

As of 9:00 A.M. on December 13, have there been more days in 1990 or hours in December?

At what time in December will the number of hours elapsed in December be the same as the number of days elapsed in 1990?

G. Years From Now

What day of the week will it be 1000 days from now?

What will the date be 1000 days from now?

H. Allowance

You are offered an unusual type of allowance: on Dec. 1 you get 1¢; on Dec. 2 you get twice this, or 2¢; on Dec. 3 you get twice this, or 4¢; and so on, all month.

Which allowance would you rather have for the month, this, or simply $100?

C. Multiples of 6

Color in all multiples of 6 or the calendar. What do you notice?

Does this happen for other months?

Do you get a pattern like this for any other numbers?

What if you try this on a hundred number chart?

D. Today's Date

You can write today's date the way it is on the calendar, but how dull!

Everyone in the class should create a different way to write today's date.

December
13
Thursday

XIII   1¢ 1¢ 10¢ 10¢

1¢   1+1+1+10

$2 \times 2 \times 2 \times 2 - 2 - 2 - \frac{2}{2}$

E. Days of the Week

In 1990, which day of the week occurs most often?

What will be the answer for 1991?

What about 1992, 1993, ...? Is there a pattern?

A. Which Digit?

Which digit (0 to 9) occurs most often in the calendar this month?

Which occurs least often?

Is the answer the same for every month of this year?

1990
December

S	M	T	W	T	F	S
						1
2	3	4	5	6	7	8
9	10	11	12	13	14	15
16	17	18	19	20	21	22
23	24	25	26	27	28	29
30	31					

B. Last Year

Last year December 13 was a Wednesday.

What day of the week was December 25 that year?

What date was the last Thursday in that month?

Commentary: 34
CALENDARS

For these challenges you can use a classroom calendar, or perhaps duplicate pages from a more convenient calendar that children can write on. The calendar can be viewed in different ways. First, it is a structured array of numbers and so can be used to pose problems related to numerals as in Challenge A or position of numbers in the array structure, as in Challenge C. Second, it measures time in a regular way, and the repeating patterns of days of the week, days of the month, months of the year, and leap years lead to many problems regarding the relationships among these patterns, as in Challenges B, E, F and G. Each day there is a new date, which can be used to generate problems related to a particular number, as in Challenge D. Finally, the partitioning of a month into days can provide a context for posing a classic problem, as in Challenge H. When appropriate, adapt the problems to the current date.

See Measurement of Time, Set 29, for some ideas related to ones in this set.

A If "1990" is shown at the top of December's calendar, "1" occurs most often, 15 times, while 4, 5, 6, 7 and 8 each appear the least often, 3 times. In any month, "1" occurs at least 14 times in this century. There may not be a "31st" day of the month. In the year 2000, some months will only have 13 "1's." You might ask students if they can imagine a month where "1" will not be the most common numeral.

B Monday. Children might do this by "brute force," that is, in a direct but time consuming way by drawing a section of December's calendar and writing in the numerals 13 to 25. The problem can also be solved by reasoning that in that month, the dates 13, 13 + 7, and 13 + 14 were all on Wednesday. If the 27th was a Wednesday, two days before, the 25th, was a Monday. Still another approach is to see that this year December 13 is on a Thursday, the day after Wednesday. Since this year December 25 is on a Tuesday, last year it must have been on the day before, a Monday. To encourage this type of thinking, specify that no pencils are to be used.

C Multiples of 6 or 3 give diagonal patterns, from lower left to upper right, on any month's calendar, from in fact on any listing of consecutive numbers in an array with 7 columns. Multiples of 4 and 8 also give diagonal patterns, but going from upper left to lower right.

This challenge can be used to launch an interesting extended investigation for children, to find which numbers yield diagonal patterns when their multiples are colored, in number arrays with different numbers of columns. An easily available array is the hundred number chart, where diagonal patterns are given by multiples of 3, 9 and 11. Children might eventually generalize that if there are N numbers in each row of an array, then all divisors of N − 1 will give diagonal patterns of multiples, and so will all divisors of N + 1. On a calendar no sets of multiples of a number (greater than 1) give vertical patterns, yet on a hundred number chart, 2, 5 and 10 do. Again, children might generalize that vertical patterns will be given by multiples of any divisor of the number of columns.

D There are no correct answers here, just room for creativity. In this challenge children tend to use whatever skills they have. You might get them started by providing a few examples which use recently developed notation or skills. If you want to ensure that students use specific skills, you can list symbols that students must use — for example, you might say that students must use both "x" and "+." You could also require that they use only 1's, or only some other digit.

E A year of 365 days consists of 52 weeks and 1 day. January 1 was a Monday in 1990, and so 1990 had 53 Mondays and 52 of each of the other days. In leap years, the first two weekdays of the year occur 53 times. As seen in Challenge B, the day of the week for a given date advances one day each year, and so in 1991 there will be 53 Tuesdays. 1992 is a leap year, and so there will be 53 of both Wednesdays and Thursdays. 1993 will have 53 Fridays.

F Students might clarify this problem — it is easiest to consider only the number of completed days in the year. The computations required to solve this problem can be simplified by shortcuts: first, since there are 365 days in the year, and on December 13 there are only 19 days left in the year (including the 13th which is only half over), then 365 − 19 = 346 days have passed in 1990 on December 13. There have been 12 x 24 = 288 hours in the first 12 days of December, and so by 9:00 A.M. on December 13, 288 + 9 = 297 hours have passed in December. To answer the second question, students might experiment to see that at the start of December 14, 347 days have passed in 1990, and 13 x 24 = 312 hours have passed in December. The hours cannot catch up with the days. But at the start of December 15, 348 days have passed in 1990 and 14 x 24 = 336 hours have passed in December. Thus 12:00 noon on December 15 is the answer.

G Students might reason that 1000 = 7 x 142 + 6. The day of the week will be the same after a number of days which is any multiple of 7, and so after 1000 days it will be the same as after 6 days, when the day of the week will be yesterday's. This challenge is related to clock arithmetic.

H This is a classic problem that can be phrased in many contexts. Look for the pattern:

$$1 + 2 = 3 = 2 \times 2 − 1;$$
$$1 + 2 + 4 = 7 = 2 \times 2 \times 2 − 1;$$
$$1 + 2 + 4 + 8 = 15 = 2 \times 2 \times 2 \times 2 − 1.$$

An easier way to write this is $2^4 − 1$. The allowance, in cents, at the end of 31 days will be $2^{31} − 1$, which is a very large number. To see just how large, notice that 2^{10} is a little more that 1000, and so 2^{31} is equal to 2^{10} x 2^{10} x 2^{10} x 2 which is more than 1000 x 1000 x 1000 x 2 = 2 billion. Thus the allowance would be more than 20 million dollars for the month of December. Further work with large numbers can be motivated by the story, A Grain of Rice by Helena Clair Pittman, in which a young farmer is rewarded by an emperor by this pattern of grains of rice, doubled for each space on a chessboard. The reward is greater than what the emperor can produce.

CHALLENGE SET : 35

children's literature

Mathematics can be found in everything. Literature is no exception. There is mathematics in plots of books, in their page set-up, in the time it takes us to read them, in their date of copyright, in the amount it costs us to buy them. These challenges give a few examples.

Next time you read a book, see what mathematical ideas you are using.

A. Caps for Sale—A Riddle

The peddler has 8 caps.

There are more blacks than reds.

There are 2 more reds than whites.

There are just these 3 colors.

What hats is he wearing?

B. Copyright

In your class book collection, which author has the most books?

To find out when the books were written, look for the copyright date. Over how long a time were these books written?

C. Book Order Forms

Suppose you have $15.00 to spend. What books would you choose from the current book order form if you want the greatest number of books? the greatest number of pages? the books you like best?

D. Heartbeats and Witches

In the chapter "The Heartbeat of a Mouse," in Roald Dahl's book *The Witches*, the grandmother tells the mouse-boy that a mouse's heart beats 500 times a minute.

How many times more does the mouse's heart beat in an hour than yours?

E. Bookworm in Narnia

The seven paperback volumes of *The Chronicles of Narnia* by C.S. Lewis are arranged in order on a bookshelf. Each book is 1.3 cm thick. A hungry bookworm starts at page 1 of Volume 1 (*The Lion, the Witch and the Wardrobe*) and eats straight through to the last page of Volume 7 (*The Last Battle*). How far did the bookworm go?

F. Alice in Wonderland

Alice finds that drinking from a little bottle makes her shrink to 1/3 of her height, and eating a cake makes her stretch to 2 times her height.

What happens to her height if she drinks a bottle, eats 2 cakes, then drinks another bottle?

How can she get back to normal height?

G. How Long Does It Take?

Pick a favorite magazine. Without actually reading it, how could you estimate how long it takes to read it, cover to cover? (You can skip the advertisements.)

How much time would it take you to read every issue of a yearly subscription?

H. Gulliver's Travels

Gulliver measured the belt of a Lilliputian and found it to be 3 inches long (not counting the overlap).

How tall was this Lilliputian?

One of the standards in the Curriculum and Evaluation Standards for School Mathematics proposed by the National Council of Teachers of Mathematics is that of "Mathematical Connections." At all levels, mathematical ways of thinking should be applied to other curriculum areas. Interdisciplinary connections between science and mathematics are commonly recognized (through measurement, expression of relationships in graphs and formulas). Also Social Studies clearly uses mathematical tools when collecting, analyzing and displaying data. Perhaps the links between mathematics and literature are less obvious to teachers and students.

The challenges in this set are intended to illustrate some of the ways in which connections can be made between mathematics and children's literature. Sometimes the plot of a book suggests a manipulative as in Challenge A, or a context for formulating new problems as in Challenges D, F and H. The book itself has physical dimensions as in Challenge E, costs a certain amount as in Challenge B and takes a certain time to read as in Challenge C, was written at a certain time as in Challenge G. You can doubtless use books that students are currently reading in many of these ways. Once students have seen a few ways in which story lines can relate to mathematics, challenge them to come up with more mathematical connections in books that they enjoy reading. See the booklet, How to Use Children's Literature to Teach Mathematics by Rosamond Welchman-Tischler (NCTM, 1992), for more complete description of types of uses, and for detailed lesson plans for specific books.

A This challenge refers to the classic *Caps for Sale* by Esther Slobodkina (Scholastic, 1984), in which a peddler sells caps of varied colors that he carries neatly on top of this head. This is an example of how the context of a book can be used to phrase problems. Children should have caps to manipulate to work out this riddle. Excellent caps can be made by spray painting dried lima beans. (See the article "Children's Literature and Mathematics," by Rosamond Welchman-Tischler in the February, 1988, issue of *The Arithmetic Teacher* for more ideas of how to use this book to teach mathematics.)

B Looking at the copyright dates of books is an interesting way to use number skills, and at the same time think about how an author's work develops, and what books have in common. Likely authors are Tomi DiPaola, Dr. Seuss, Arnold Lobel, Beverly Cleary. Chapter 8 of the NCTM booklet, *How to Use Children's Literature to Teach Mathematics*, mentioned above discusses this and other ways of looking at an author study with a "mathematical eye."

C School book club order forms are free and can be given to children even if they are not expected to order books. This challenge illustrates one possible use of the forms. You might also ask about how to get the greatest savings if there are many books on sale, or how to have the least amount of money left over. Challenge students to write other mathematical problems arising from the book order form.

There are other examples of free printed sources of real-world numerical data that can be distributed to all children in the class for them to use to solve problems and make up new ones. Consider using supermarket handouts, take-out menus from restaurants, timetables, and charts of rates for telephone calls or postage.

D This challenge refers to *The Witches*, a book by Roald Dahl, who often incorporates significant mathematical content in his stories. This issue of heartbeats is interesting because in another book by Dahl, *Matilda*, different data is given, namely that a mouse's heart beats at the rate of 650 times a *second*. This is so far off from the rate in *The Witches* that it probably should have been the rate per *minute*. This raises the question of whether both figures, 500 and 650, could be correct for pulse rate per minute? Students can collect data about their pulse rates in different circumstances — while sitting in a well-rested state or after running around the playground. How can one compare the differences? Dahl's *Matilda* figure is 30% higher than his *Witches* figure. Do students' pulses differ by the same percentage?

E This is a classic "trick" problem. One might assume that the worm must eat through all 7 books, going from page 1 of the first to the last page of the 7th, so the answer should be 7 x 1.3 cm. However look at how the books are arranged on the shelf. The worm needs to eat through only the covers of the first and last books, and so the answer is 5 x 1.3 (plus the thickness of four covers, which is very small since the books are paperbacks).

F The effect on her original height will be to multiply first by 1/3, then by 2, by 2 again, and by 1/3. The result is to multiply height by 4/9. Unless Alice finds a new magic potion, or takes fractional parts of the bottle or cake, she can never get back to her original size exactly, because the result of any number of ingestions is of the form $2^n/3^m$. For no powers n and m can 2^n be equal to 3^m. (The "Fundamental Theorem of Arithmetic" states that any number can be factored into primes in just one way.) However, Alice can get close to her original size. $2^8/3^5$ = $256/243$ = 1.05, and $2^{11}/3^7$ = 2048/2187 = .94. Students can find closer approximations on a calculator.

G This challenge can pull in many mathematical topics. If students are only going to read text, not advertisements, they might measure area of actual text, then time themselves on sample.

H Students can measure some sample adults and find the average ratio of waist to height. (Often waist is a little less than one half of height, and so the Lilliputian was probably a little more than 6 inches tall.) A nice related activity is a "Lost and Found." Present, say a toy car or a doll's cup, or a bracelet (which looks like a ring) and say "Someone has lost her car [or cup, ring, etc.]. How tall is she?" The idea behind this challenge can also be interpreted in terms of many other books involving change of size.